What's Your Name?

Other Books by Louis Adamic

KOBOTCHNIK·VALJAVEC·CHAPMAN·SWITALSKI

WHAT'S
YOUR NAME?

BY

Louis Adamic

HARPER & BROTHERS PUBLISHERS

NEW YORK AND LONDON

ROOSEVELT·SCHUYLER·KRZYZANOWSKI·HOUGHTELLING·BIALOBLOSNKI

HICKS·ADAMOPOULOS·PODLESNIK·COHEN

SWANSON·VISHNEVETSKY·UNDERWOOD·PAPADEMETRACOPOULOS

To

CARLTON E. MORSE

and his

"PAUL BARBOUR" (MICHAEL RAFFETTO) OF
ONE MAN'S FAMILY

This publication was made possible in part by funds granted during 1939–41 by the Carnegie Corporation of New York. That Corporation is not, however, the author, owner, publisher or proprietor of this publication, and is not to be understood as approving by virtue of its grant any of the statements made or views expressed herein.

Contents

PREFACE

WITH the rest of the world, we Americans find ourselves neck-deep in the exigence of our times. It is forcing the complexities of our civilization to new highs—and the end is not in sight.

For about two years now, since the fall of France, but particularly since Pearl Harbor, we have taken many steps calculated to meet the onrushing, unpredictable future. Among other things, we as individuals have been lining up and registering and reporting for all sorts of things.

We are filling out all sorts of forms—applications, questionnaires, statements, depositions. We are required to show birth certificates and other documents attesting to our beginnings. We must have rationing cards. We are obliged to appear before boards and commissions in sudden authority over certain matters pertaining at once to our personal existence and to the national emergency.

Right and left, we are being asked, "What's your name?"

In June, 1941, in *This Week* magazine, Sunday supplement of a number of large newspapers, I published the short story of Kobotchnik and his dog Nurmi which is the first chapter in this book. In April, 1942, I received a letter signed Joseph Pedrotti:

I am twenty years of age and a 1941 graduate of ———— College here in Pennsylvania. The week I graduated I chanced to read your article about Kobotchnik, not realizing at the moment that I would soon be faced by a problem akin to his. . . .

In school I prepared to become a teacher (French, Latin, English) and last summer I entered my application for a vacancy with a nearby prep school for boys. With helpful recommendation from the college I managed to secure an interview with the headmaster who was very nice and seemed well pleased with my qualifications. From his talk I gathered the job was mine; we discussed salary, what was expected of me, etc. Next week he would write me a letter confirming the substance of our conversation, and then he would expect to see me early in September.

I waited for his letter, but none came for ten days, three weeks, almost a month. Finally I wrote to him. No reply. Then I heard from the —— College Alumni secretary who said he had had a long conference with the headmaster concerning me. (The headmaster is an alumnus too.) It seemed there was the "little problem" of my last name. Could I change Pedrotti to Peters, or something similar? If I did that, the appointment was mine.

"I am sure you will agree," read the letter, "that although they have distinguished themselves in many other fields, the Italians have not done so well in education. Mr. H—— [the headmaster], therefore, feels that the parents of the boys in his school would take exception to an Italian name on the faculty. . . . Your qualifications far outrank those of the other applicants, and Mr. H—— hopes you will make the necessary change (a simple legal matter) and accept the position."

I was hurt. So were my father and mother and my two sisters, both schoolteachers, and good ones. I wrote the headmaster, preferring not to use a go-between as he had done, and explained that I did not want the job under that condition. I pointed out that Angelo Patri, Leonard Covello and Pestalozzi were people with Italian names distinguished in the field of education in this country. If his school objected to my Italian name because of the war and Italy's position in it, I wished him to know, I said, that my sympathies were completely with England and Russia and the occupied countries.

Mr. H—— did not answer. Later I learned that a classmate of mine, whose parents are Russian immigrants and who had Anglicized his name, was elected to fill the vacancy. But he taught only two weeks, then was called into the Army. Who followed him, I don't know.

Do you think I was foolish in refusing to change my name and thus refusing the position? I have been both praised and rebuked for my decision. Financially, the job was not worth much, although it may have been a stepping-stone to something better.

I feel perfectly all right about not getting the appointment, but I *was* a little upset. I still am—obviously, or I would not be writing to you now, after having hesitated to write for months. But I know I would have been very miserable if I had discarded "Pedrotti."

I know Italian immigrants and sons of Italian immigrants who have Anglicized their names to obtain jobs, with the result that their Italian friends and relatives look down upon them somewhat for it. My name is not so cumbersome that it is hard to spell and pronounce. Why should I be required to become Peters "or something similar"?

At present I am working in a coal mine, by my father's side, and I feel quite good about it. I think I have always nursed a secret, perhaps a little romantic, desire to work in a mine— in the same pit with my father, whom I admire and love very much. Except for the college years, I have lived in this coal town all my life.

I am helping a little with the family budget—something I could not have done, had I accepted the school job. And I am physically preparing myself for duty with the armed forces (I am slightly underweight). I registered with the Selective Service in February. I've been wondering if being Pedrotti would be a factor with me in the Army, but yesterday I took the bull by the horns and applied for an officers' training course. We'll see. I may be a success as Pedrotti yet!

But seriously: I can see that some people may think me foolish, and possibly I *should* change to Peters, "or something similar," to preclude any difficulties in the Army; all I know is that I want to hold onto my name. Why, I don't know exactly. Perhaps it is that, like Kobotchnik, I too want to be myself, and that this is somehow tied up with the fact

I have mentioned—that I do have a deep affection for my father, and his name is Pedrotti.

I don't know if "Pedrotti" will affect this young man's military career. It will depend on many things.

The Army has no official attitude toward "foreign" names, but they are, nonetheless, somewhat of a problem in our armed forces. Thousands of top sergeants find the daily roll calls one of their toughest jobs, for in some outfits half the personnel have names which are relatively difficult to pronounce. Their owners are kidded and tossed undignified nicknames. Of course they usually take it with a grin, but it affects them. Some seriously. It touches their morale. I know that many inwardly squirm and tauten against the moment when their names are called.

There is no doubt that in most outfits it is much simpler to be an Adams than an Adamciewicz. There are generals in the Army named Shekerjian and Barzynski; yet seven or eight times out of ten, if Privates Adams and Adamciewicz stack up about equally for promotion to corporal, and there is only one vacancy at the moment, the chances are in favor of Private Adams. Some of the top sergeants and platoon and company commanders, who decide these promotions, will deny there is such discrimination; yet it is true. It works subtly, unconsciously. It is apt to be all the more true when the company commander or top sergeant has a "foreign" name himself: for a man with a "foreign" name who has attained to the rank of captain or top kick often leans backward—quite unwittingly, let me emphasize—lest he give the appearance of favoring a "foreign"-named soldier.

Eventually Private Adamciewicz, if he continues to be a good soldier, is promoted too; meantime, however, he becomes a little more self-conscious about his "foreignness" than he was before. This may be a positive or a negative factor in his career as a non-com, depending on the fiber of his character and on the strands of experience in his background. It may depress him, or it may sharpen his wits and spur him on.

This is of course also true of the Navy and the Marine Corps.

And it is not new to Adamciewicz. He is an ex-civilian; and the name problem in the armed forces is but an extension of that problem as it exists in civilian life. In fact, my impression is that it is rather less serious in the Army, the Navy and the Marines than in the American atmosphere as a whole.

Our names are more important to us than ever before. And I feel this may be an excellent moment for a glance at the intricacies and absurdities pertaining to them. I should like to see the problem considered by the whole country, but particularly by schools, colleges and universities, by employers and their hiring agents, and by those in charge of morale in the armed forces, as well as by other officers and men.

LOUIS ADAMIC

Mountain View Farm
Milford, New Jersey
Mid-June 1942

The Importance of Being Kobotchnik

Where a man calls himself by a name which is not his name he is telling a falsehood.

LORD ESHER, *Judgment in Reddaway*
vs. Banham, 1895

A MAN AND HIS DOG

THE little news story, under a New England dateline, told of an immigrant who thirty-seven years before had changed his name from Kobotchnik to Cabot because his wife and daughters were ashamed of his old-country name, and who was petitioning the local court to restore it to him. His daughters were married; he was a widower, old and alone, and he wanted to fulfill the wish of more than half his lifetime to be Kobotchnik again.

A few months later, curious about the man, I made it a point to look him up. His petition had been granted. He was a meek-looking little fellow with a wizened old Slavic face. He had left the New England town where he was known as Cabot; now he lived in retirement by himself, batching, in a small house on the edge of another New England town. Although not a well man, he was enjoying—with a glum, unsmiling Coolidgean humor—the fact that he was Kobotchnik again. He spoke with a New England twang mixed with a foreign accent, and I found him eager to talk about his name.

I asked him what difference it made whether one was called Cabot or Kobotchnik.

For a moment he looked at me in helpless silence. Then:

"What difference it makes! To me it makes this difference: now I am happy! I feel like a new man—no, I didn't mean it that way. I feel like I was before I changed my name to Cabot; only maybe more so. I have a bad case of asthma, I'm old, and I'm going to die soon, but inside—here," putting a hand over his heart, "I feel young. I sure do. Young.

3

"What difference it makes! As Cabot, I was not happy. How could I be? I'm *not* Cabot," he shot out. "Sometimes while my name was Cabot, I had crazy ideas—and some maybe were not so crazy. I thought of walking away and never coming back to my family again. Once I saw a man do that in a movie. He just walked off! I had other crazy ideas that I don't want to tell you about, they was so crazy. Well, I can tell you one more. I was gonna get all the money I could and go—just go—back to the old country, where I could be Kobotchnik again.

"I was born a Russian. I come from the Carpathian Mountains. If that's not the best place to come from, I'm sorry, I can't help it, but that's where I come from; so my name is Kobotchnik. I feel good now. When I was Cabot, I felt awful—like a dog I once had.

"Let me tell you about that dog. I got him from a Finn who has a farm outside of Fitchburg. He was about a year old then, this dog, and he had a name. He was just a mutt, but a wonderful dog, very fast; he liked to run, so the Finn called him Nurmi—after the Finnish runner that the farmer was very proud of. He got very attached to me, I mean Nurmi, the dog, and I was crazy about him.

"We had him about a year . . . and he was two years old, when my wife and daughters decided they didn't like his name. Their argument was: Who ever heard of a dog called Nurmi? What if he was named after the Finnish runner! This ain't Finland, this is America, ain't it? That's how they talked. To tell you the truth, I never was much good at arguing, least of all with my wife; so she and the girls started to call the dog Buster. They yelled at him, 'Buster! Buster!'

"They liked the dog, all right, but they was dumb. Women! The dog was smart, but he couldn't figure 'em out; he didn't know what to make of them. They didn't call him Nurmi any more. 'Buster! Buster!' He *wasn't* Buster, and I guess when they called him that, he thought they was scolding him. This was terrible for Nurmi, because there was never a friendlier dog. He behaved well, and wanted to be liked. Now: 'Buster! Buster!' all the time. . . .

"Well, in a couple of months he looked like he was going to pieces. I'm not exaggerating, I sure am not. He didn't run any more. His tail was down most of the time. He was nervous and jumpy. His nose was warm. It was summertime, but he shivered like he was cold. He let out little squeals. He was afraid to bark. What kind of a dog's life was that? I ask you!

"When I was alone with him, I called him Nurmi, and he would of like to go crazy, he was so happy all of a sudden. But I knew my wife. She was O.K., only stubborn as they come. She thought whatever come to her head was right, and if she decided to put her idea over on the world, nothing could stop her. She was foreign-born too, but come over as a child. When she grew up, she got ashamed of being a 'foreigner' and wanted to be 'American.' She wanted the girls to be 'American.' She thought nobody who amounted to anything would marry 'em if their name was Kobotchnik; so *I* had to become Cabot. I had to turn into a fake Yankee. I ain't got nothing against Yankees, you understand. I just didn't like to pretend I was one, what with this accent and my coming from the Carpathian Mountains. I don't like anything fake. That's how I am; I'm sorry, I can't help it. . . .

"Anyhow, I knew my wife would keep on calling the dog Buster, and so would the girls, because while I was working in the woolen mill for twenty-nine years, she raised 'em so they paid no attention to me and listened to her; and I figured it wasn't fair for me to call him Nurmi any more. It only made things worse for him. He would never get used to being Buster. I thought maybe that if I started to call him Buster too, by-and-by the poor mutt would resign as Nurmi and become Buster—just like I resigned as Kobotchnik and became Cabot.

"I was never more wrong in my life. Me calling him Buster didn't help at all. He was getting more miserable right along, so my wife and daughters stopped liking him. They thought he was no good and a nuisance. And he really wasn't very pleasant to have around. He just wasn't himself.

"I took him to a dog doctor and got some pills. He was supposed to have distemper. The medicine didn't help. He was just a mutt, like I told you; I got him for nothing; but I was sorry for him as could be.

"Then he disappeared. No sign of him for three, four days; a week. I thought he was run over, and I said to myself: His troubles is over. But I was sad. Next I got the notion that maybe he just run away. I hoped that was what happened. But after a while I wasn't sure if a dog was smart enough to clear out like that. I thought only the fellow in the movie and I were so bright to get the idea to walk off.

"I was wrong again. About a month after the dog disappeared, I was in Fitchburg one afternoon, and who yelled at me from his car by the curb but the Finn that give me the dog. He said, 'Hey, Mr. Cabot!'—my name was still Cabot then; this happened about ten years ago.

"The Finn told me my dog come back to him. Nurmi was alive! He went back on the farm where he was born. I never thought he would do that. It was thirty-one miles away.

"Was I glad! I was so glad I could of cried. I asked the Finn how Nurmi was. Was he all right? The Finn told me he was kinda funny when he first come back, but he was fine now. He was catching all the rabbits on the place. He was a regular terror with the rabbits and squirrels and ground hogs.

"I went over to the Finn's farm, and sure enough, there

was my dog, my Nurmi, running around like his old self
again—only in no time I could see he wasn't my dog, my
Nurmi, any more. When he first saw me, he barked at me;
then, for a little while, he looked scared and miserable
like he was before he disappeared, and he squealed and
cringed on the ground. I couldn't see him good because
I had tears in my eyes. I said, 'Hello, Nurmi! Hello,
Nurmi!' I tried to pat him on his head like I used to. But
all of a sudden he growled and jumped up like a shot, and
he snapped at me. He never done that before. I pulled my
hand away quick, just in time, or he would of got me.
Then he barked at me from a distance, till I left. If I made
a move toward him, he might of bitten me. How he barked
and growled! And I can't tell you how I felt. I felt pretty
bad. He hated me. Nurmi had no use for me any more.
I was his enemy.

"I understood him perfectly. Who *would* understand
him if *I* didn't? Now, back on the Finn's farm where he
was born, everybody called him Nurmi. Nobody yelled
'Buster! Buster!' at him. He was himself again. He was
happy. . . .

"The Finn looked at me hard. He thought I come to
take the dog back again. But when he saw how Nurmi
acted, he asked me angry-like if I ever kicked him. I said
no, of course not; why should I kick him? He was a good
dog. Besides I never kick any dog. I like dogs. I explained
to the Finn what happened: that my wife wanted to call
him Buster and he didn't want to be Buster, so he run
away, and now he was angry. I said I didn't blame him for
not wanting to be Buster. He was Nurmi. I didn't blame
him for being sore at me, either. I didn't stick by him. I
wanted him to resign as Nurmi, like I resigned as
Kobotchnik.

"The Finn laughed like he was fit to bust. 'Sure he's
Nurmi,' he said. 'Buster! What kinda name is that for a

dog that was born on a farm owned by a Finn and can run like he can? He's Nurmi!'

"I agreed. I said he better keep Nurmi, and the Finn understood. I left the dog there, and never felt worse in my life. Then I got the idea I told you about: to clear out and go back to the old country, like Nurmi went back to where he come from. Only I didn't have Nurmi's guts. I had a family. . . . That was about ten years ago. Long time. . . .

"Now everything's all right. I'm Kobotchnik. I like America, sure; I like New England. I guess that's why I stayed here. I'm here more than forty years now. Why shouldn't I like America? The country's all right; I'm crazy about it; it's just some people are wrong and ball up other people. . . . It's a free country, ain't it? If a man's name is Kobotchnik he should be Kobotchnik; why not? And if he wants to, he can call his dog Nurmi; why not?

"Sure, I'm an American citizen. I become a citizen thirty-five years ago under the name of Cabot, but that was fixed up. I'm an American citizen under my real name now: Kobotchnik. And I have another dog; he was just a pup when I got him, and hadn't got any name yet; so I call him Nurmi!"

My Own Name

Men are the constant dupes of names, while their happiness and wellbeing mainly depend on things.

J. Fenimore Cooper, *The American Democrat,* xlvi, 1838

THE AMERICANIZATION OF "ADAMIČ"

ORIGINALLY in my native Carniola (or Slovenia) my surname sported a tiny hook over the *c*—thus: Adamič. It was pronounced Ah-dah'mitch, with both *a*'s long and full, the accent on the middle syllable, and a sizzling *tch-ch-ch* at the end as in "pitch." Literally "Little Adam" or "son of Adam," it is the Slovenian equivalent of Adamson or Adams.

In my earliest years in the United States (1913-15), as a very young greenhorn eager to be "Americanized," I occasionally spelled my name Adamich or Adamitch. For a time, when I was about sixteen and picking up the English language from newspaper headlines and from the speech and signs in New York streets, I considered changing it to Adamage, the way most Americans pronounced it when they saw it written with the *ch* or *tch*. This idea came to me on hearing of an immigrant named Savič who had "Americanized" himself into Savage. But I rejected it when I learned of another immigrant who had Anglicized his name from Garbič to Garbage, and when I realized that "damage" was not much more attractive a word than "garbage."

I was probably not as attached to the old-country spelling of my name as to its sound, which had been familiar since childhood. But this is stating the thing a bit too simply.

I was bent on becoming an American. At the same time I was instinctively proud—in an indefinite, fluctuating way—of being Adamič. In Carniola, ours was a numerous clan which had no more than the average proportion of misdemeanants and ne'er-do-wells, and a few people of our name had mildly distinguished themselves in Slovenian history. A leading contemporary Slovenian composer was Emil Adamič. And shortly before my departure for the United States a young man named Ivan Adamič, a relative of mine, had been killed by the Austrian military in a Yugoslav-nationalist student demonstration in the streets of Ljubljana, the provincial capital. He was thereafter a kind of martyr-hero to large sections of the Slovenian nation, and his picture draped in black crepe hung in homes all over the country.

Partly because he had been killed so dramatically and partly because he had been Adamič, this martyr-hero played quite a role in my mental and emotional processes in America. He was subtly instrumental in rousing my enthusiasm for President Wilson's idea to make the world safe for democracy and he had, I suspect, a good deal to do with my joining the United States Army. And very possibly it was the memory of him that prodded me into signing my application for enlistment as Adamič with a disproportionately large hook over the *c*.

But that was as far as the *č* got in the Army. The typewriter on which my service record was made out did not have it; the clerk either ignored it or thought it was an accidental scratch of the pen; and the spelling of my name in America was determined then and there. I became Adamic, was so naturalized while in the Army, and have so remained.

In the Army my Americanized name usually appeared at the head of every alphabetical roster. There was no question about its pronunciation. I was called Ad'amic, with the stress on the first syllable and the middle *a* barely heard.

I had then been in the United States a little over three years and my attachment to the original sound of my name had gradually weakened. For all I know, in spite of my one-time satisfaction over its significance in Slovenia, I may even have developed a subconscious discomfort about the spelling and sound of "Adamič." It may be that my service in the Army superseded in importance everything before it. At any rate, it occurred to me that Ad'amic sounded better than would any possible articulation by English-speaking tongues of Adamich, Adamitch or Adamage.

Some years after the war, while looking through a fat Webster's in a public library one day, I encountered the word "Adamic," which meant "pertaining to Adam." The discovery that my de-hooked Slovenian cognomen was an English adjective gave me an amused pleasure, which a further discovery dampened a little. Webster declared the correct pronunciation of the word to be A-dam'ic, which, compared to Ad'amic, seemed awkward.

But this had no practical bearing at the time—1921 or 1922. No one with whom I came in contact knew the word that meant "pertaining to Adam," and, as in the Army, I was invariably called Ad'amic.

Since the early 1930's, however, considerable confusion has developed about my patronymic. Each time a book of mine appears inquiries come from librarians, booksellers, and lecturing book reviewers as to its "correct" pronunciation. Going about the country, I hear myself called A-dam'ic almost as often as Ad'amic. To inquiries I reply in spite of Webster that I prefer Ad'amic but am willing to let the pronunciation establish itself.

I believe Webster is wrong about the pronunciation of the word which means "pertaining to Adam." Most educated English-speaking people, I know, follow his directions, but I think were the word to come into general usage the masses of people, who have little respect for linguistics but a proclivity for rhythmic speech, which in English tends to place the accent as near the beginning of the word as possible, would pronounce it Ad'amic and eventually old Noah's successors would have to catch up.

There is another factor. During the later 1930's a number of Americans who happen to have read a book of mine called *The Native's Return* visited Yugoslavia, where they heard that my name was "really" Adamič, and they spread the word among others in their communities who were interested in such information. In this they were aided and abetted by a New York literary friend of mine who once gave my name his version of its old-country pronunciation over a national radio hookup; and, too, by my Yugoslav fellow immigrants scattered over the American continent. For years now the book-readers among them have engaged in lively arguments with librarians and booksellers, insisting I am neither Ad'amic nor A-dam'ic but Ah-dah'mitch, which non-Slavic tongues usually transform into Odd-ahm'eesh.

But this is not all. In recent years I have been taken to task by a number of intellectuals among my Slavic fellow immigrants for allowing my name to be amended. Mr. Victor J. Valjavec, a native of Slovenia and a passionate American with a long career as an official on Ellis Island, once wrote me in a faintly censuring tone that I should have insisted on retaining the Slovenian č. He suggested that it was not too late for me to regain the hook.

I should follow, he said, the example of Dr. Aleš Hrdlička, the famous Czech American curator of the Division of Physical Anthropology at the Smithsonian Institution in Washington, who did not permit his name to be "spoiled" by English orthography. When he saw it written Alesh Hrdlichka (its approximate Czech pronunciation) he demanded *h*-lessness and the restoration of the hooks. Since then, Mr. Valjavec told me in words charged with triumph, the United States Government Printing Office has spelled it "correctly"—Aleš Hrdlička—and some other publishers have properly followed suit.

Mr. Valjavec's own name is no easy matter for non-Slavic tongues. It is difficult to write so the average American will pronounce it with Slovenian correctness; the closest I can come is Vah-lyah'vets; but he does not regret all the effort and patience he has devoted in the last forty-odd years to preventing its verbal murder in America. Its root is the Slovenian verb *valjati*, "to roll"; and the fact that one of his relatives renamed himself Rollington is a source of some unhappiness to him. He believes that all we Americans of Slavic derivation need is Doctor Hrdlička's strength of character.

"At the time of the Spanish-American War," says Mr. Valjavec, "the English-language newspapers in the United States never used the Spanish letter ñ, which is pronounced 'ny,' as in *mañana*. But Puerto Ricans, Cubans, Mexicans, and nationals of other Latin American lands insisted on it in the press of this country as a matter of courtesy to the Spanish alphabet which is at least as old as the English; and from about 1905 on important newspapers, magazines, and book authors and publishers have taken good care to use ñ. . . . Slavic literatures may not be as old as either Spanish or English, but there are about 200,000,000 Slavs in the world, and I ask: why can't we Slavic Americans expect the č, š, and ž in our names to be accorded the same respect in the United States as that given the Spanish ñ? . . ."

In common with other Slavic Americans who have criticized the Americanization of my name, Mr. Valjavec has—good-naturedly enough, but firmly—dismissed my explanation as irrelevant. He maintains that as an American writer of Slavic origin I owe it to my fellow Slavic Americans to join Doctor Hrdlička in his admirable stand and restore my name to Adamič.

But except for people like Mr. Valjavec I find little encouragement to follow the Hrdlička example. I note in fact that the renowned anthropologist's cause shows scant promise of success. He appears to be giving up the fight. Possibly he realizes that the odds against the original Bohemian spelling are hopeless. He is listed as Aleš Hrdlička in the English *Who's Who*, while *Who's Who in America* in common with practically all other English-language publications in the United States has him down simply as Ales Hrdlicka—which leads people to pronounce it almost like "hard liquor."

It is all very well for Mr. Valjavec to be impressed—for his own subjective reasons—with Doctor Hrdlička's attitude, but he should also consider the principle involved. As a world-important scientist, Doctor Hrdlička is in a position to require the United States Government Printing Office to spell his name as he pleases. But an ordinary Civil Service clerk cannot address any such request to anyone in Washington. And so it seems to me the question arises: Is it fair, in a democracy, for Doctor Hrdlička to have this advantage over the average-run person? Perhaps as fair as the economic advantage a millionaire has over the majority of people. And also one wonders what would happen if the other foreign-born in advantageous positions should insist on old-country spellings. For instance, would it be all right for Spyros Skouras, president of the Twentieth Century-Fox film company, to require us all, Mr. Valjavec included, to write his name

ΣΠΥΡΟΣ ΣΚΟΥΡΑΣ

as it was written in Greece? If so, then it would be logical for all of us to learn to write Sholem Asch's name in Yiddish,

שלום אש

and Lin Yutang's in Chinese characters,

As for the parallelism between the Slavic č and the Spanish ñ, Mr. Valjavec should not forget that nearly all the countries in the Western Hemisphere are more or less Spanish (not Slavic) in language and culture; that Mexico (and not Slovcnia, Poland, or Bohemia) borders on the United States; that New Mexico is basically a Spanish-speaking state; that Puerto Rico (and not Bulgaria or Slovakia) is a territory of the United States; and that it is therefore more natural for North Americans to respect the ñ than the č. I notice, however, that the ñ too receives pretty rough treatment by even the most "important" U. S. American publishers.

On the other hand, although Adamic is not really difficult and is a recognized English word, old-stock Americans have complained that I have not gone far enough in "Americanizing" it. A New York gentleman named Chapman wrote to me early in 1941 that he did not know where the accent fell (which apparently caused him to resent me a little), and that to prove the sincerity of my expressed desire for unity in this country I should set an example to "other foreigners" by renaming myself Adams—"a good American name."

"There may still be some Adamses left in England," says Mr. Chapman, "but I have never heard of one. . . . 'Adams' is common in the United States, and you should be as willing to adopt it as people named Depuis long ago were willing to be called Depew, or those named Huet, Hewitt. . . . This is an English-speaking country; a country where the Anglo-Saxon vehicle for the amalgamation of a new nation got a head-start . . . and names here should be spelled so they can be easily pronounced by millions of people whose oral mechanism has long been conditioned by the English language."

I have no intention of heeding either Mr. Valjavec, who attaches so much importance to linguistic symbols, or Mr. Chapman. They uphold two extremes which to my mind are about equally wrong. Each represents a large opinion, Mr. Chapman perhaps the larger. Except for the preceding paragraphs, this chapter is not meant to be a direct reply to them; I mention their views simply because they come into the story of my own name.

I decided to tell that story not because my case is important or bothers me but because it is the closest at hand. I could hardly avoid it in this book. Also I think it suggests a number of elements typical of the name problem in contemporary America.

In its many-faceted totality this problem virtually amounts to a sort of psychological or cultural battle which is being waged over most of the United States and whose issue is not one of "foreign" names alone. Names are but the most obvious aspect, the surface summation, of a complexity of subtle "Plymouth Rock and Ellis Island" difficulties, real and imagined, which often go deep.

To some of us the battle over names is not at all serious. It scarcely touches us and we shake off its effects as ducks shed water. For others it is acute. It impinges on their everyday life, and many are unable to extricate themselves either by doing something about it or by viewing it philosophically.

I think I am not callous to censure. Nor am I indifferent to the confusion over the "correct" pronunciation of my

Americanized name. I too am involved in the problem, but it does not disturb me because I have given it what thought I could and have in recent years worked out a few pieces of an idea about names that rather suit me and take care of what nuisance mine might otherwise cause me.

I shall not try to pack these bits of an idea into a few neat, compact, dogmatic paragraphs. There is nothing neat, compact or dogmatic about them; in fact some almost contradict others. They will appear here and there through this book.

TOWARD ORGANIC CHANGING

NAMES are a device of convenience—a comparatively recent one at that. Fundamentally and objectively, that is all they are—a device to introduce order into the maze of human relationships, a means of distinguishing you from me.

In the course of time, many names passing from parents to children have acquired much subjective significance. This is true not only of famous names; it is true of "Kobotchnik" as well as of "Cabot." Actually though, in most cases, in most places, and most of the time, *if* one could be sensible about it, it should not much matter what one's name is.

But that "if" up there is a tremendous little word.

One should be a person rather than a name. Too many honored names have not been made or earned by the people who now bear them. They have merely been inherited. One has no moral right to exploit a name which someone else has enriched with weight and honor, and thus to assume a vicarious importance. It is likely to be fatal to one's character; and personally I consider that people afflicted with such names who lack the extraordinary ability required to infuse them with a new significance might do well by themselves and society if they adopted others.

Take "Randolph," for example. It is a highly honored name in Virginia and elsewhere in the United States. Much history attaches to it. There are many Randolphs, and many of them, of course, are real, effective human beings. But one of my acquaintance is obviously and completely devoid of any quality which might make *him* significant. He is as mediocre as are some of the Rupniks, Ronattos and Robinskys I know. Performing no useful function of any kind, he is primarily a name walking or riding about. Yet he has great pretensions which rest on the achievements of his ancestors. He is a child of the past, fiercely identified with it, desperately devoted to it. When I was last in touch with him, he was an alien-baiter and a professional patriot without the faintest comprehension —literally—of contemporary America. He is on the defensive against the present and the future. All the vitality he manifests rotates about the significance of his great name. Were it taken away, there would be next to nothing left of him—as he now is, at any rate. The cherished, elaborately constructed illusion that he is a man of parts would dissipate; even his possessions would be unable to keep it going.

After such a catastrophe, one might conceivably seize the opportunity to become a human being and build up a new significance under a name not famous. But it would scarcely be possible for the Randolph I know. He is the prisoner of his name. Middle-aged, he is hopelessly enmeshed in the thick, entangled subjectiveness that goes with spurious importance. He is snobbishly happy about being a name instead of a man—although, of course, he would not put it that way.

What applies to "Randolph" goes for less illustrious and so less stifling names; and not only in America. Had I remained in my native country, I would have had no right to whatever significance attaches to "Adamič" in Slovenian history—although I probably would have tried to assume some, judging by my feelings back in 1914 and 1915. And, since I emigrated, I have even less claim to its Slovenian significance. So why should I put up a fight for its old-country sound and spelling? Why should I bother about the hook over the *c*?

I think I have become during the last twenty-nine years progressively less Slovenian and more American. I have, however, not become an Anglo-Saxon American. I couldn't, for I lived my first fifteen years in Slovenia. I have become a new kind of American, a Slovenian American (without the hyphen; "Slovenian" is an adjective here), and it seems to me that, since for convenience's sake I must have a name, Adamic is a logical tag for me. It is an American revision of my hereditary name, as I am an American revision of the boy who left Carniola in 1913. I am a different human being than I would have been had I never left Europe, and I cannot bring myself to lament this or to mourn for the little jigger over the *c*. In my opinion, Adamič became Adamic *organically* while I was becoming an American; which is pretty much as it should be.

I stress the word *"organically"* because the change in my name occurred without deliberation on anybody's part. There was no issue. I yielded to no pressure. I was subjected to none. The hook just disappeared. Naturally. Inevitably. By joining the United States Army I moved into a strictly English-speaking atmosphere in which hooks over *c*'s would have been a considerable nuisance in the midst of more weighty business than the spelling of a name.

I suppose I could have insisted on the retention of the hook, but that would have been inorganic. It would have manifested Slovenian nationalism, which has no discernible long-range relevance in the New World. It would have been as if I now suddenly yielded to either Mr. Valjavec or Mr. Chapman, both of whom are out deliberately to create an issue. It would be as inorganic as if I were to revert to the *č* or change to Adams, or dictate arbitrarily the current pronunciation of my name.

By this I do not mean there should be no deliberate changing of "foreign" names. Sometimes the reason for it has to be regarded as organic. Certain non-English names are objectionable in an English-speaking country and should be changed no matter how. (More of this later on.) But usually a natural, accidental, casual or organic alteration, as I have shown with my own cognomen and as I shall further illustrate, is preferable to an unnatural one impelled by force and fear.

My view is that almost anything organic is better than anything which is not. (By "organic" I mean—briefly— that which comes about mainly of itself with very little inner conflict; which grows or emerges naturally out of an undistorted interrelation among all the pertinent circumstances.)

Obviously this notion has evolved out of my own experience. Perhaps it is a rationalization. Very well; the point is that it settles the matter for me. And it may aid others. It may even partly disarm such warriors in the battle of names as Mr. Valjavec and Mr. Chapman in whose cross fire are currently caught the majority of the nearly five million aliens, eight and a half million foreign-born citizens and thirty or forty million native-American sons and daughters of immigrants whose names are relatively "foreign" or difficult, and who are either reaching for weapons or looking for exits from the conflict.

There is no easy exit for any large number of the "foreign"-named. I favor declaring a truce in the battle and asking what the shooting is all about. Today, as suggested in the Preface, the name problem is more widespread in the United States than ever before. On many sides it is acute, bitter. Sometimes Anglicization does little good. Sometimes it does positive harm. Once in a while it may be the organic solution; the name practically Anglicizes itself.

But the struggle which is being waged goes deeper than names.

American Names: Long Ago and Now

The glory and the nothing of a name.
>BYRON, *Churchill's Grave*, 1916

The nothing of a name.
>POE, *Tamerlane*, viii, 1827

BEGINNING WITH APOLLOS RIVOIRE

SOME two hundred years ago Apollos Rivoire, a Huguenot immigrant from the Isle of Guernsey in the English Channel, changed his name to Paul Revere—"merely on account that the bumpkins pronounce it easier." Perhaps Deborah Hitchbourn, who married him soon after (and became the mother of *the* Paul Revere), had had something to do with it.

At any rate, it was no uncommon practice. "The English language," says Sabine Baring-Gould in *Family Names and Their Stories*, "is impatient of foreign sounds, and insists on rounding or roughing them into some semblance to a known English word, as 'Shovell' out of 'Escoville.'" And Howard F. Barker, author of the American Council of Learned Societies' significant study, *National Stocks in the Population of the United States as Indicated by Surnames in the Census of 1790*, is impressed by "the abrasion of common speech."

There is, however, some basis for supposing that name-changing was not a sport Paul Revere, Sr., always approved; in his will he cut off his grandson "Frank, who now signs his name Francis," with one dollar.

Other French names were modified before the War of Independence. Comberford, for example, became plain Comfort. I have a friend named Popenoe whose original Huguenot family name was Papineau. Franklin Delano Roosevelt's middle name came to him from his mother, Sara Delano Roosevelt, a descendant of Phillipe De la Noye, who came from a Huguenot family of Leyden, Holland; the name was subsequently simplified by jamming it into a single word: Delano. The intrepid Bon

Coeur became Bunker, giving his name to Bunker Hill, according to Captain Marryat's Diary, although the Massachusetts historian Dr. S. E. Morison claims the famous hill really got its name from George Bunker, an early English immigrant. Petit was changed to Poteet, Caillé to Kyle, Guizot to Gosset, Soulé to Sewell, Gervaise to Jarvis, Fontaine to Fountain, Denis to Denny, Pibaudière to Peabody, Bon Pas to Bumpus, and so on.

The same thing happened with German names. My late friend John Fearhake's first American ancestor was a pre-Revolutionary immigrant glass-blower from Germany named Feuerhacke. General John J. Pershing descends from a German named Friedrich Pfoersching who arrived in Pennsylvania in 1747, while Schwab was the original name of some of the Swopes. The Indian fighter, General Custer, was a descendant of a Hessian mercenary named Kuester who was paroled after Burgoyne's surrender; and A. B. Faust says in his great work, *The German Element in the United States,* that even that famous American name, Lincoln, may have been originally German—Linkhorn. Hoff was Anglicized into Hough, Huber into Hoover, Roggenfelder into Rockefeller, Pfeffer into Pepper, Knoebel into Noble, Koch into Cook or Cox or Coke, Baumann or Bachmann into Baughman or Boughman or Bowman, Bauer into Bower, Bischoff into Bishop, Fischer into Fisher, Fuchs into Fox, Guth into Good or Goode, Haas into Hays, Heintz into Hinds or Hynes, Jung into Young, Klein into Clyne, Kohl into Cole, Poh or Pfau into Poe, Neumann into Newman, Pfeiffer into Piper, Volch into Foulke, and Weil into Wylie. Many German names were literally translated. In Pennsylvania many Carpenters stem from immigrants named Zimmermann; while Pfund was changed to Pound, Schumacher to Shoemaker, Koenig into King, Schaefer to Shepherd or Sheppard, Meister to Master or Masters, Kurtz to Short, Weber to Weaver, Braun to Brown.

The names of Swedes and Swedish-Finns who came over in the early eighteenth century to settle on the Delaware were altered too. One of them, Kyy, was changed by degrees to Kyyn to Kyn to Keen, while John Morton, one of the signers of the Declaration of Independence, had a Finnish grandfather whose original Old-World name was Marthinen. The late Albert P. Terhune's name was originally Finnish: Terhunen.

The Dutch in New York City and up the Hudson Valley —the Van Rensselaers, Stuyvesants, Roosevelts, Ten Eycks, and Schuylers—resisted name-changing more than any other non-Anglo-Saxon group. They were particularly successful where they were economically entrenched before the Anglo-Saxon strain invaded the region, and well enough educated so they could spell their names consistently. But in the case of the Dutch, too, Kuiper became Cooper; Van de Veer, Vandiver; Reiger, Riker; Haerlen, Harland; Prins, Prince; Hoogsteen, Highstone; Veldhuis, Fieldhouse; Zilvernagel, Silvernail; Koning, King. Some of the translations were exact, some free.

This was nothing new. H. L. Mencken—from whose fourth revised edition of *The American Language* ("Proper Names in America," pp. 474-554, an amazing compilation of information) I take with his leave much of my data—says:

Changes in surnames go on in all countries, and at all times. They are effected very largely by transliteration or translation. Thus the name Taaffe, familiar in Austrian history, had an Irish prototype, probably Taft. General Demikof, one of the Russian commanders at the battle of Zorndorf, in 1758, was a Swede born Themicoud, and no doubt the founder of the house in Sweden was a Frenchman. Edvard Grieg, the Norwegian composer, had a Scotch forefather named Craig. Franz Maria von Thugut, the Austrian diplomatist, was a member of an Italian Tyrolese family named Tunicotto. This became Thunichgut (do no good) in Austria, and was changed to

Thugut (do good) to bring it into greater accord with its possessor's deserts. In Bonaparte the Italian *buon(o)* became the French *bon*. The family is said to have come from Southern Greece to Corsica, and to have been named Kalomeris originally. Of this, Buonaparte was simply an Italian translation. Many familiar English surnames are Anglicized forms of Norman-French names, for examples, Sidney from St. Denis, Divver from De Vere, Bridgewater from Burgh de Walter, Garnett from Guarinot, and Seymour from Saint-Maure. A large number of so-called Irish names are similarly the products of rough-and-ready transliterations of Gaelic patronymics, for example, Findlay from Fionnlagh, Dermott from Diarmuid, and McLane from Mac Illethiain. In the United States, with a language of peculiar vowel-sounds and even consonant-sounds struggling against a foreign invasion unmatched for strength and variety, such changes have been far more numerous than across the ocean, and the legal rule of *idem sonans* is of much wider utility than anywhere else in the world. If it were not for that rule there would be endless difficulties for the Wises whose grandfathers were Weisses, and the Leonards born Leonhards, Leonhardts or Lehnerts, and the Manneys who descend and inherit from Le Maines.

The changing of German, Dutch and French names before the Revolution was in all probability fairly organic. It was not forced by advantageously placed Anglo-Saxon Americans, but came about casually, in ways incidental to the rough-and-tumble of life in the New World. It just happened. Before dictionaries came into use in the last quarter of the eighteenth century, spelling was not very important. Like words in general, names were mostly sounds, not arrangements of symbols on paper. They circulated by word of mouth, and when writing began to come into wider practice, they were recorded phonetically —often by public scribes or professional letter-writers, according to English orthography as they knew it.

This was no less true of Anglo-Saxon names than of "foreign" ones. A correspondent of mine, Mr. D. W.

Blakeslee of Pittsburgh, is aware of four different spellings of his family name, which goes back three hundred years in America to a number of related emigrants from England who were most probably illiterate and whose names were written down by clerks with differing orthographic ideas. And in England itself at that time even those who could write were not sure about spelling. A man who once did some research at the British Museum tells me he frequently came upon letters written in the eighteenth century by comparatively well-educated people who spelled their signatures variously at various times.

In addition to illiteracy and unstandardized spelling in those early days, many appellations coming from Britain were caught in a process similar to that of "rounding and roughing" the French, German and Hollander names. The "abrasion of common speech" worked on them, too. Baring-Gould mentions that "the well-known publishing firm of Lippincott in Philadelphia derives [its name] from an emigrant to America called Luffincott, from a small parish in Devon." In both America and England the tendency was to trim long, cumbersome names and to clip even those which were not awkward. Thus in America Desborough was abbreviated to Disbrow, Haynesworth to Haynes or Worth, Caldwallader to Caldwell, Amythill to Antill, Davies to Davis, Rodgers to Rogers, Conhope to Connop, Gaddesby to Gadsby, and Cornhill to Cornell. President Polk's ancestral name was Pollock. Thousands of English names have been altered in America since they first crossed the Atlantic.

The records of people's experiences with their "foreign" names in the Colonial period and the early decades of the United States are extremely scant. All I can be fairly sure of is that difficulties existed. But I have a mass of more recent data.

GENERAL KRZYZANOWSKI AND SOME CONTEMPORARY POLISH AMERICANS

WLODZIMIERZ KRZYZANOWSKI, a political refugee from Austrian Poland, arrived in the United States in the 1850's. His name was pronounced Vuo-jeem'yesh Kshi-zhannoff'skee.

At the outbreak of the Civil War he enlisted as a private in the Union Army and with bravery and extraordinary competence swiftly advanced to the rank of colonel and the command of a regiment of Danish, German, Polish and Russian immigrants serving under General Schurz. Most of his non-Polish soldiers referred to him as "Kriz" or "the Colonel." At Bull Run he distinguished himself as commander of a brigade, whereupon, on the recommendation of Generals Schurz and Grant, President Lincoln nominated him for promotion to brigadier general. But the nomination got entangled in the political machinations of the Senate Military Committee and was not reported out. Some of the machinations were anti-Lincoln, others issued from Know-Nothingism. The senatorial semi-public explanation, however, was that none of the Senators was able to pronounce "Krzyzanowski." The nomination later was resubmitted and confirmed, and General Krzyzanowski became the first United States governor of Alaska.

In the spring of 1939 I spoke to a group of Polish Americans, most of them college graduates, in a large eastern city. During the discussion period I was asked (as I invariably am by someone in any Polish American audience) what I thought of changing Polish names; and because his picture as a very handsome Union officer hung on

the wall behind me I told the story of Wlodzimierz Krzyzanowski, although I knew it was well known to most in
my audience. (I was not sure that I pronounced his name
quite as I should have, and felt a little uneasy.)

Then, not without suspecting that I was near a hornets'
nest, I suggested it might be advisable to simplify those
Polish names which non-Polish Americans found difficult
—as it would be advisable, I hastened to add, to simplify
Greek, Lithuanian, Croatian, Slovenian, Serbian, Ukrainian, Czech, Slovak, Italian, Hungarian, Armenian, Jewish,
Syrian, Finnish, and all other names which were jaw-
breakers to the average American. I said, however, that as
a general rule such names need not and should not be
translated or transliterated into English; their original
character, or some semblance of it, ought to be retained.
By way of illustration, I told of a man I knew in Chicago
who had—to my mind, sensibly—modified his name from
Sleszynski to Slesinski "because the 'szy' was a stumbling-
block to all non-Poles." I mentioned too the well-known
New York Polish American, Stephen Mizwa, head of the
Kosciuszko Foundation, whose name had been originally
Mierzwa, and the famous actress Helena Modjeska and her
equally famous engineer-son Ralph Modjeski whose orig-
inal name was Modrzejewski.

There was a little applause. A few people seemed to
agree with me. The chairman asked the audience if there
were any more questions.

A tense young man shot up. Clipping off his words in
a sharp tone, he begged permission to speak; he meant to
ask me several questions. He said his name was Krzyzanowski too, and he was a grand-nephew of the man whose
picture hung on the wall. Then he tore into me with hot,
eloquent indignation. On the basis of my none too successful pronunciation of "Krzyzanowski" he assumed that I
considered the name "difficult." Did I mean to suggest, he
demanded, that his grand-uncle General Wlodzimierz

Krzyzanowski should have "simplified" it? If so, would it interest me to learn that President Lincoln and Generals Grant and Schurz had never felt free to make such a suggestion to General Krzyzanowski? And why not? Because they were men of taste. They were considerate of others. They would have thought it tactless and presumptuous to suggest anything of the sort.

How would I have "simplified" it? demanded Mr. Krzyzanowski. And while we were on the subject, would I have wanted Pulaski and Kosciuszko to "simplify" their names? He desired to state that it had never occurred to their Commander-in-Chief, General George Washington, to so affront them. And why not? George Washington was a gentleman! George Washington knew that by virtue of everything in them "Pulaski" and "Kosciuszko" were *their* names. While here I was, Mr. Krzyzanowski continued with cold fury, telling a gathering of American Poles to "simplify" their names! Did I wish to advise him personally to change the name which Abraham Lincoln and Ulysses S. Grant respected and honored? To what? To Smith or Kent or Rice or Brown or Jones? Or would I prefer shortening it to Kryz or Kriz or Chris, or Zyzanowsky, Zanowski or Nowski? How many syllables would I like him to discard? And how would I decide which I wanted to retain?

Did I not realize that by favoring modification of "foreign" names I was yielding to the worst element in the United States—to the stupid, provincial, narrow, egocentric Americans, so-called, of the older strains; to people like those United States Senators in the sixties who had refused to confirm the promotion of General Krzyzanowski because of their anti-foreign prejudice; to persons who were psychologically closer to Hitler and Mussolini than to Lincoln and Washington!

If he "simplified" his name, Mr. Krzyzanowski went on, he would be catering to those Americans who were too lazy to attempt to pronounce it. Have not millions of Polish immigrants been obliged to learn such difficult names as Houghtelling, Willoughby, Dwight, Hughes, Maugham, Cholmondeley, Postlethwaite, and Cavanaugh? Instead of giving Polish Americans such advice why didn't I go around to old-stock Americans—the D.A.R.'s, say, or the Colonial Dames—and tell them to snap out of their Anglo-Saxon smugness and learn how to pronounce Polish names, which were also American? Why didn't I tell them what they should have known long ago: that Poles were with Captain Smith at Jamestown and played an important role in saving the Colony? Why didn't I tell them to stop monopolizing American history and to accept Pulaski, Kosciuszko and Krzyzanowski as important figures therein? They ought to get used to respecting Polish Americans and their Polish names, even if at first glance they did look a little "difficult."

Mr. Krzyzanowski sat down amid a burst of applause. Everybody had listened to his dramatic remarks with taut attention. Some of the same people who had agreed with me five minutes earlier now seemed either to agree with him or to like the passion of his utterance. I was expected to reply. Should I try to point out that he resembled the smug, old-stock, Anglo-Saxon Americans he condemned? That he was not unlike the Randolph I knew in Virginia?

I was considering this while the chairman was beating about the bush for me, remarking at some length that all Poles and Polish Americans were proud of General Wlodzimierz Krzyzanowski. Then, since the meeting was small and informal, I decided to ask how many people in the audience agreed with the implication of Mr. Krzyzanowski's questions. Four or five hands went up with no "maybe" about them, and one or two somewhat uncertainly. How many disagreed? One young man raised his hand, and I made a note of him in my mind. How many did not know what to think? One hand almost went up, but didn't. It looked as though the rest of the audience did not want to commit itself—yet.

I asked the young man who had disagreed with Mr. Krzyzanowski if he would care to say something.

He hesitated; then, to my relief, he answered, "Yes." He said his name was Belby, and he was a native American of Russian and Polish parentage. But once upon a time, he added, his name had been Bialoblonski.

"It's all very well," he went on, "for Mr. Krzyzanowski to stand up for the name which was distinguished in the United States by his grand-uncle. Personally, I think Mr. Krzyzanowski should not change to Jones or shorten to Zanowski, even if not one American in a thousand knows about General Krzyzanowski. At least, I don't think I would give it up if it were my name, even if I had to spend a lot of time telling the world how to pronounce it. It must be something to have an important name when one isn't very much—I am speaking of myself now. I think too that anybody in the United States who happens to be Pulaski or Kosciuszko or Modjeski should retain his name. They are accepted by the educated in this country as names in American history, although I don't doubt they are not stressed enough, particularly in schools attended by a lot of youngsters of Polish parentage. Also if one's name should happen to be Paderewski, one should remain Paderewski."

Mr. Belby continued:

"It's a different kettle of fish, though, when your name is not distinguished and the question before you is, 'Little man, what now?' Till I was twenty-two Bialoblonski was a constant embarrassment to me. I was always regarded as a 'foreigner' in spite of my American birth. In college it kept me out of fraternities. Once, after a girl had introduced me to her family, her mother told her not to have anything to do with me. I know this is all crazy, but it was

serious enough then. I could tell you three or four other
experiences which were hard to take although now I can
recall them with some detachment.

"When I looked for work, I had to spell my name over
and over again, and I knew from the employment manager's expression that I would not be taken on. I needed
a job more than anything else, and . . . well, I was up
against hard facts of life and human nature, which no
romantic notion about one's name could contravert.

"Then I was hired in spite of my name. It seemed almost too good to be true.

"A few weeks later my boss gave me a fatherly talking-to.
I should change my name. He himself, of Czech and German blood, had translated his from Kovacs to Smith. He
was sure that with his original name he would never have
been able to develop his business, and he predicted I
would not get very far as Bialoblonski. I would always be
regarded as a 'Rooshen' or a 'Polack' or a Jew, but if I
adopted some 'simple name' he would train me to become
a buyer. He liked me, he said, but he could not afford to
send me around the country as a representative of his firm
under the name of Bialoblonski.

"I could not tell him—and the world—that a grand-
uncle of mine, General Bialoblonski, had fought with
Ulysses S. Grant in the Civil War ——"

Several people laughed out loud and the audience began
to relax.

"I couldn't say," Mr. Belby resumed, "that I was specially proud of my name. As a matter of fact, I wasn't. It
was a pain-in-the-neck.

"Since *bialo* means 'white,' I thought of calling myself
White or Whitehouse. But when I broached it to my
folks, a storm broke out. 'Bialoblonski' did not mean
much to my mother, but it did to my father. He said if I
dropped it he never wanted to see me again. He did not

speak to me for a week. But Mother worked on him, and in the end we settled on Belby."

Laughter.

I did not have to say anything more that evening. Touched off by Messrs. Krzyzanowski and Belby, people needed little encouragement to talk about their names. Some said they had no difficulty—"or," in the next breath, "almost none." One maintained that most of the "name trouble" was imagined. The majority, however, told of experiences and inner perplexities that sounded very real. And while all the statements were highly subjective, together they gradually restored the audience to a balanced attitude.

"My name used to be Paczkowski," said a young lady, "which to non-Poles was a tongue-twister. I had to spell it endlessly, but people often misunderstood me and wrote it down wrong. Once I was refused a job because the employer assumed I was Jewish. People used to laugh at my name; I heard remarks like, 'Well, she's a Polack!' This hurt; it seemed so unfriendly and as though people of Polish blood were inferior! . . . One day when I was ordering something by mail, I just couldn't write 'Paczkowski,' so I put down 'Pace.' I was not home when the package came, and there was trouble that night at supper. My parents are proud of being Polish, and I had to promise them I would never do it again. Then," she added, "I married a man named Sunbury. His name used to be something like Sonofski; he isn't even sure how it was spelled. Neither of us is ashamed of our Polish descent, but it is much simpler to be Mrs. Sunbury than Mrs. Sonofski or Miss Paczkowski."

Another young woman said: "My parents' name is Kopankiewicz. My older brother was called Copey at school, which was all right with him and he went into the Navy as Copey. My younger brother is still Kopankiewicz.

On the whole, we had no trouble worth mentioning when we were children. We lived in a Polish neighborhood and went to school with other boys and girls of Polish parentage. . . . In business college, though, I was advised to change my name, but I didn't. I knew my father wouldn't like it, although he probably would not say anything. I got a job in the filing office of the Mid-town Department Store. The manager called everybody else Miss So-and-so but called me just Josephine. . . . Then I applied for a job in the Junior Misses department, where girls are paid better. They told me bluntly there was only one thing against me: a girl called Miss Kopankiewicz could not work at a counter, where customers might ask her for her name. . . . Our family likes to read, and we are all very proud of Joseph Conrad, whose original Polish name was Josef Konrad Korzeniowski; so I became Josephine Conrad—but only on the job; otherwise I stick to Kopankiewicz."

The editor of a Polish-language paper recalled the term "consciousness of kind" originated by the sociologist Giddings. "People like to recognize others of the same derivation, and names help. That is why readers who stick to their Polish names write in to my paper every week denouncing people who Anglicize theirs. Not that I condemn the latter, but I understand too those who retain their old names. All over the country are Polish Americans named Young and Smith and Williams; they are doing good work or even important work, but we don't know about it; if we knew they were of our stock, it would help us in our hours of trouble. When we hear that Mr. Simpson, the engineer building this bridge or that dam, is really the son of an immigrant called Szczypiorski, a thrill comes to us. Polish papers print the news and Polish Americans everywhere feel a little better about themselves, but at the same time a little uneasy because young Szczypiorski had felt obliged to become Simpson.

"Some years ago a ship sank in mid-Atlantic and another ship rescued its crew and passengers. The captain of the rescuing ship was hailed as a hero. In the Associated and United Press dispatches his name was given as Captain Michaels, but I knew he was the son of my late friend Majchrowicz; it did my heart good to read about his heroism. I published his identity in our paper and then I received a lot of letters from readers, thanking me for the information. But all of us regretted that the big English-language papers in New York and Chicago and Buffalo and Detroit and elsewhere reported only the Anglicized form of the hero's name. It would have meant so much to us all if the American public knew that one of our kind had done a brave deed."

Someone told the ancient joke about the Irish policeman who found a drunk on the corner of Second Avenue and Kosciuszko Street. The cop could not pronounce "Kosciuszko" so he carried the drunk a block to Second Avenue and Lafayette Street before he called the station for the patrol wagon.

Still another young woman said: "In high school, I was almost never Helen Golembiovski but 'that Polish girl.' For a while I tried to tell people I was an American, born here; it did no good. My brother had trouble too; nothing very serious, but unpleasant. Sometimes boys would yell after him, 'Johnny Golembiovski—give 'im a kick in the pantski!' We didn't change our name and we try to be philosophical about annoyances. My sister, who married a Polish American with a name even 'worse' than ours, feels the same way. We can take it. I think some day names like Golembiovski and Derensky will be as respected in America as Pulaski and Paderewski. When we new Americans get over our 'foreigner' inferiority complex, there are going to be great artists, writers, scientists, engineers and political leaders with such names—lots of them—and then it will be a great thing to be Golembiovski or Derensky, and cops won't move drunks when they find them on Kosciuszko Street."

Applause and laughter.

"Meantime," Miss Golembiovski went on, "all we need is a little backbone. I think I agree with Mr. Krzyzanowski, although now and then I weaken and feel tolerant toward people who modify their names. But I think this sort of thing is encouraging: I know two American-born men of Polish descent who six or eight years ago Anglicized their names—one from Baroszewicz to Barton, the other from Kowalczyk to Smith. For a while they were a little more comfortable, but not much happier—names are a funny thing. Then they began to be impressed by what they heard about Poland. One of them read Eve Curie's biography of her mother. . . . Well, Mr. Smith has already changed his name part way back—to Kowal—and Barton is seriously thinking of doing the same thing."

A middle-aged man with a heavy, melancholy face and a slight accent announced, bowing to Miss Golembiovski in the Old-World manner, that he too meant to keep the "difficult" name he had brought to America thirty-odd years ago. "It has," he said, "a sort of mystic personal significance to me, which perhaps only those of Polish heritage can fully understand. It has value as a cultural and nostalgic tie to Poland. Who of any sensitivity would deny me this? The bother I have had spelling my name and teaching people to pronounce it only served to enhance that value and deepen that significance."

The gentleman broke off, thinking. As we waited for him to go on, there wasn't a sound in the room.

"Alas," he continued, "many Americans born here of Polish parentage are unhappy, uneasy about their names.

As some of you have suggested, this is all wrong, but perhaps it is beyond our power as individuals or as Polish Americans to right in time to do any good. In fact, nearly everything that has been said here tonight makes me sad. I am a citizen of the United States. I love America as I love Poland—more than Poland (some of you will know what I mean); but I am confused. There is a pain in me. One of my brother's sons Anglicized his name before he entered the Military Academy at West Point, which was created by a Pole, Kosciuszko! I was miserable about this because in the old country only criminals change their names. It was not required of my nephew; he simply thought it would help him, although in the last ten years a good many young Americans of Polish descent have graduated from the Academy without discarding their parents' names."

He paused again, then:

"I have a friend who once called himself Grzywaczewski, an old honored Polish name. He is now Gary. He lives far from this city; none of you know him; and so I can talk of him. His son was called John G. and was given his diploma, with apologies by the principal, as John G. Nobody tried to pronounce his last name. The boy was brilliant and wanted to go to Princeton. He aspired to teach in a college. One of the daughters had difficulties too. For years there was a perpetual family crisis on account of the name. So now after much agony the whole family were renamed Gary. Personally, I am sorry, but who am I to blame my friend Grzywaczewski or my nephew at West Point?"

A distinguished-looking man rose briefly to remark in an impersonal voice that the dropping of "foreign" names for English ones was "social mimicry." Except in unusual circumstances it should not be approved. It indicated a tendency to conformity which was "childish—and perhaps un-American if Longfellow's and Thoreau's ideas on nonconformism may be regarded as part of Americanism."

NAMES ARE ENMESHED IN A MAZE OF OTHER PROBLEMS

WHAT is true of Polish names applies to Czech, Slovak, Serbian, Croatian, Slovenian, Russian, Ukrainian, Lithuanian, Rumanian, Greek, Jewish, Finnish, Hungarian, Italian, Spanish (including Mexican, Cuban, etc.), Portuguese, Armenian, and Syrian and to some Norwegian, Swedish, Danish, Hollander, German, French (also French-Canadian) and Belgian patronymics. There is a great jumble of tendencies. Some are headed by various routes in the same general direction, others go in the opposite direction by the same and other routes. I know of no short-cut to making the subject clear.

I expose myself, I know, to a suspicion of complicacy. Especially apt to suspect me will be those who have encountered the problem only in passing. But it *is* extremely complicated. I have been looking into it hoping to find it simple and easy. I wish it could be isolated. But it is enmeshed in the maze of greater problems.

A few of its simpler, more obvious factors have already been suggested. Some of the others are obscure and not easy to present.

One is a kind of hangover from the struggles of primitive man to establish his identity, importance and niche in a chaotic, mysterious, inimical world. ("The development of civilized thought," said Alfred North Whitehead in his *Modes of Thought*, "can be described as the discovery of identities amid diversity.")

There is also the general human inability to see oneself objectively in relation to people, processes and problems.

There are the effects of nationalism, whose rise scholars connect with the study of language, and to which has been ascribed much of contemporary man's sensitive self-consciousness.

These considerations affect the matter of names in most countries. Then we have the broad, overlapping conditions of American life which add their complications. I shall mention only the most important.

There is the haphazard "Americanization" or assimilation movement, popularly referred to as the Melting Pot, with its spasmodic environmental and individual drives and strains.

There is the country's cultural atmosphere, crisscrossed with prejudices, usually vague but sometimes sharply focused, which people of different backgrounds hold against one another. Some of the prejudices are perfectly natural and intrinsically sound tensions, antipathies and camouflages for group-protective purposes; but since the diversity within human America is so great they operate negatively on too huge a number of individuals to achieve any positive national results.

There is economics. Our financial and industrial ups and downs, playing on the attitude of old-stock Americans toward the new stocks, greatly affect immigrants and their American-born children. The majority are still "marginal and acutely exposed."

And we must not forget the backwash from the developments in the Old World during the last thirty years which, slopping over on the United States, have been sharpening up already divergent attitudes.

Important too are the previously mentioned demands of English speech and orthography. These demands are especially strong in America. In England we still find no end of long or "funny" names. In the British *Who's Who* occur Edward W. Billyard-Leake, Ernest Tom Neathercoat, Rita Francis Mosscockle, Worsfold Mowll, Maxwell Homfray Maxwell-Gumbleton, Geoffrey Rupert Cecil Twisleton-Wykeham-Fiennes, and Joshua Whatmough. The name of the present British Ambassador in Turkey is Sir Hughe Montgomery Knatchbull-Hugessen. In the United States the trend is clearly toward simplification. "Many a monosyllabic American surname of today," wrote *The Literary Digest* of September 21, 1918, "was a gaudy roll of syllables a century ago."

No less weighty is the still prevalent concept that fundamentally the North American civilization is Anglo-Saxon. In certain salient ways this is undoubtedly true. But often it is too dogmatically maintained or too insistently implied, rousing resentments and defenses in non-Anglo-Saxon Americans, who are conscious of their groups' contributions to the sum-total of the United States.

These are the circumstances, the weapons, the elements, the issues, the lineup of the psychological civil war of which the battle of names is the most obvious part.

The whole business is highly subjective. The Polish American meeting was an unusual occurrence. The audience, as I have indicated, consisted mostly of educated, articulate people; but even the articulate in new-immigrant groups are not often disposed to discuss their difficulties so concretely in public—even when no "Americans" are present.

Usually when the subject comes up in public, many dismiss it, too insistently, as unimportant. Others are incapable of any frankness about it even in private—or within themselves. To some who come in contact with "Americans," especially if they have attained to the pretensions of professional or white-collar status, the name problem is a very delicate matter. It reaches into the tender recesses of their personalities, or it would if they let it. This is likely to be true whether the "foreign" name is changed or not, *if* a disproportionate amount of conviction, stubbornness or indecision is involved. It is all mixed up with a sense of inferiority on the part of millions of immigrants and their native-American children. For they are still deep in the process of adjusting themselves to America, itself a process of a most dynamic and furious kind, not too well understood even by the most advanced old-stock Americans.

It is difficult for Americans generally, whether new- or old-stock, to realize that nothing is yet settled or permanent in the New World, least of all its human composition. The American Revolution is still going on in more ways than one.

MANY CHANGE THEM IN VARIOUS WAYS

DURING the last fifty years great numbers of immigrants with non-Anglo-Saxon backgrounds and greater numbers of their American-born children have changed their names. Many have made extreme alterations. Later I shall show that the tendency has been diminishing since the early 1930's, especially since 1941, but it is still strong. Many names are literally or freely translated into English—as Marangopoulos (Greek) into Carpenter; Zelenjak (Slovenian) and Zalionis (Lithuanian) into Green; Yerganian (Armenian) into Long; Kirkkomäki (Finnish) into Churchill; Krejči (Czech) or Szabó (Hungarian) into Taylor; Bienvenue (French-Canadian) into Welcome; Piekarz (Polish) into Baker; Gutjahr (German) into Seasongood or Goodyear; and Weiss and Schwartz (usually Jewish) into White and Black. To one who knows both English and the old-country language, some translations are amusing. In my native land, for instance, Podlesnik is a common name (*Pod* meaning "under" and *les,* "wood"); and when I come upon former Podlesniks in this country who now are Underwoods, I can smile to myself all day. I see something funny also in the fact that the father of the notorious evangelist Billy Sunday was a German immigrant named Sonntag. And I have laughed over Jean Baptiste Trudeau in Drummond's French-Canadian dialect poem who became John B. Waterhole.

Some literal translations are more awkward than the originals; some approach the ridiculous. A man whose name used to be Riesental now calls himself Giantvalley, presumably to conceal his German descent. And I have heard of a Thousandfriends and a Turnipseed, probably also direct translations of old-country names.

Many transliterate their "foreign" patronymics, whether "difficult" or not, into phonetically approximate English names—Huttunen and Kolehmainen (both Finnish) into Hutton and Coleman; Mikalauskas (Lithuanian) into Mc-Closkey; Coumoutzis (Greek) into Cummings; Bojtić (Croatian) into Boyd; Ctrnacty (Slovak) into Sterns; Brocco (Italian) into Brock; Kosanović (Serbian) into Cousins; Kukman and Svetec (Slovenian) into Cook and Sweets; and Jakše or Jakšič (also Slovenian) into Jackson. Some transliterations too are a little comic, such as Bucci and Neri (both Italian) into Buckeye and Neareye, and Klobučar (Slovenian) into Clotsbutcher.

English or pseudo-English forms are sometimes achieved by phonetically transforming only portions of the "foreign" names—as Matulaitis, Kruzentaitis and Liskauskas (all Lithuanian) into Late, Cruse and Luskey; Schwetten-dieck (Dutch or German) into Dick; Cohen into Conn or Coyne, and even Cain, Cowan, Cole or Calhoun; Zaharić and Hrvatin (Croatian) into Zachary and Harvey; and Mihajlović (Serbian) into Michael or Mittchell. Al Simmons, the renowned ballplayer, was originally Aloysius Szymanski.

Most changes have a story behind them. Rabbi Sanders A. Tofield of Houston, Texas, says: "Even many Jews could not pronounce our family name of Tofilovsky. . . . Father finally agreed to change it, but we children could not concur in any of the proposed substitutes. . . . Traveling, I used to look up names beginning with *Tof* in telephone directories all over the United States. No luck. Then I happened to go to Canada and in the Montreal directory I came upon 'Tofield,' which was acceptable to the whole family."

Most people when they change want to retain in the new name the initials of the old. The November 3, 1941,

Time magazine reported: "In Jersey City, Michael, Helen, Joan, Joseph, Walter, Sophia and John Rozmyslaws won permission to change their name to Roosevelt."

The problem is most acute for those with "difficult" names who leave or have never inhabited the "foreign" sections, and for those who do not wish to cut away entirely from their immigrant background but whose ambitions take them to school or to work in the big "American" world where they come into close contact with "Americans," or who are drafted into the Army. A "foreign" name handicaps them in most pursuits outside the "foreign" colonies, and they stumble or fall into one tendency or another. Not a few abbreviate or otherwise simplify their cognomens without trying to make them sound English. Many Greek Americans now named Pappas were once Papadopoulos, Papanicolaous, Papageorgiou or Papademetracopoulos. A Lithuanian American of my acquaintance who was once Andziulatis is now Andjel. Finnish names have been shortened from Hietakangas to Kangas, Hirvisalo to Salo, Ruonovaara to Ruono, and Eckonen to Eck. An Austrian American dropped the middle syllable in Kotlechner, becoming Kotchner, a Slovenian American started in life as Zakrajšek and now is simply Zak, and several Armenian Americans have lopped the *ian* off the end of their names. I know an Italian American whose family name, Lapiscarella, he changed to Carrell, while his two brothers simplified it, one into Lapick, the other into Papick—the *P* being due to the court typist's error!

An American of Lithuanian parentage, Edward Le Vanda, writes: "When he came to the United States, my father's name was Levandauskas. It was always mispronounced and often misspelled. Father finally consulted a lawyer, and they decided to saw off a good part of the awkward 'handle' and make it Levanda; but the judge who heard the petition suggested turning the small *v* into a capital; capital *V* it became, and our family has been Le Vanda ever since."

This, incidentally, is an example of the sort of advice people burdened with the "foreign"-name problem are likely to have inflicted on them by those in positions of prestige who could exercise much desirable influence if they took the trouble to give it some thought and become informed about it. Levanda is a sensible alternative; why destroy its Lithuanian characteristic by giving it a French twist?

Poles and Polish Americans seem impelled to more name-changing than any other group. In the Detroit area with some 300,000 of them, about 3000 modify their names every year. Why and how they change them, and what they go through before and after the change, has already been suggested.

Jews—with the exception of the small Sephardic group who are proud of their cognomens—apparently experience the least inner difficulty in renaming themselves. A good part of the explanation lies in their Old-World background. In some countries their ancestors were required less than a century ago to choose names which were easier to remember and pronounce for the rest of the population; in others, notably in Germany, new names were simply assigned to them. Then too they sometimes changed their names as a tactic against anti-Semitism. Most Jewish surnames are not Yiddish or Hebrew, but Spanish, German, Italian, Polish, Dutch, and so on. Thus, compared with a great many Gentiles whose current names go back, they like to think, for many centuries, a large majority of Jews have no strong cognominal traditions and attachments. With many, when they came to America, alteration was almost a matter of course. I have mentioned what some of the Cohens do; other Cohens, in New England, have become Cabots or Cabbotts, although some Yankee

Cabots tried to stop them with court injunctions. Many Levys have renamed themselves Levitt, LeVie, Levay, Lowell, and Lee. Some of the one-time Wolfsohns are Wilsons; Blumenthals, Bloomingdales; Rogowskys, Rogerses; and Jacobovskys, Jacksons. Thousands of Stones in the directories all over America are former Steins and Weinsteins and Finkelsteins. A Jewish friend of mine whose name now is as "American" as Dewey or Brooks said to me that with his old Jewish name on his business stationery "handicaps were stacked up against me before people saw me." Mencken says that probably half the Jews of New York "now sport new names," including Adams, Lincoln, Harrison, Jefferson, Vanderbilt, Gould, Schuyler—and even MacGregor. Some of the translations of Jews' names are amusing: for instance, Edelstein into Noblestone.

Unlike most Gentile groups and like the Jews, the early Norwegian immigrants too had no firm cognominal adherence. Even now among the common folk in Norway it is not unusual for the son to take his father's first name —Hans, say—and become Hansen or Hanson; while his sister assumes the surname of Hansdotter (Hans's daughter) and keeps it even after marriage. On coming to the American Northwest, Norwegians discovered that old-stock Americans and German, Czech and other immigrant settlers confused them with Danes and Swedes, many of whom had identical or else very similar names; whereupon, to quote from a footnote in O. E. Rölvaag's *Giants in the Earth*, "their slumbering sense of historical fitness awoke," and many "adopted the name of the place they came from in the old country." These new names, usually ending in *-dahl, -fjeld, -gaard,* and *-stad,* were harder to pronounce than Hansen, Olsen, Johnson and other such tags they had brought to America, but the changes prevented some confusion all around and no little ire on the part of Norwegians who did not want to be taken for Swedes or Danes.

Swedes, when they began to come over in large numbers, had name troubles similar to the Norwegians', and others besides. Many, says Mencken, "really had no surnames, in our sense of the word. The son of Johan Karlsson was not Lars Karlsson but Lars Johansson, and Lars' son Johan in his turn was simply the son of Karl." Swedes, thus, had a rather unusual patronymic tradition which easily permitted Jonsson to become Johnson; Swensson, Swanson; Olsson, Olson; Karlsson, Carlson; Andersson, Anderson; Petersson, Peterson, and so on, till the country was so full of Johnsons, Swansons, Olsons, Carlsons, Andersons and Petersons that they could not be singled out. In his very interesting book *The Religious Aspects of Swedish Immigration*, Professor George M. Stephenson, of the University of Minnesota, gives amusing examples of how this problem was solved: "John Johnson in the employ of Mr. Green was called John Green to distinguish him from another John Johnson; the John Carlson who had gone with the gold rush to California was nicknamed California Carlson. The portly Albert Swanson was called Albert Fat Swanson, and the Peter Anderson whose house was set back some distance from the road was designated Pete-in-the-Street. John G. Princell, the religious leader, was the son of Magnus Gudmundson, who changed his name to Gummeson in America. Princell took his name from Princeton, Ill." Charles A. Lindbergh's family name was originally Mansson.

The problem of Scandinavian names was acute from Michigan to Oregon in lumber and construction camps where bosses solved it by numbering the Ole Olsons I, II, III, IV, or—if they themselves happened to be non-Scandinavians and lacked a full measure of respect for Scandinavian names—by arbitrarily changing them. Thus inflicted on the immigrants, some of the new cognomens stuck. There are Scandinavian American families in Minnesota and Wisconsin named Sullivan, Smith and Riley. In St.

Paul, one Anders Olson switched to Olson Anders. Comparatively rare are such grand-sounding names as that of a Norwegian American friend of mine, Björgluv Björnaara, who has a farm outside the little town of Trail, Minnesota. Many Olsons, Johnsons, Andersons, and Swansons have relabeled themselves everything from Lincoln to Davis and from Lee to Grant.

But even so there are myriad Johnsons, Andersons, Petersons and Petersens, Olsons and Olsens, Hansons and Hansens, and Swansons, which results in frequent confusion. In the Twin Cities every once in a while post-office clerks get frantic, as do others obliged to deal with names: librarians, teachers, draft and rationing board officials. It is doubly bewildering because Scandinavians also have common preferences for first names. At one time a good part of Minneapolis seemed to consist of Ole Olsons.

The "foreign"-name situation contains complex personal and communal difficulties and contrasts.

It appears that the educated Jew with a Polish, Russian or German background "Americanizes" his name more readily than his uneducated brother. His greater social and cultural adroitness, his enhanced sensitiveness to anti-Semitism, his wider mingling with Gentiles lessen still more the slight cognominal tradition shared by the uneducated Jew.

Some educated Gentile immigrants whose names are "difficult" feel much the same way. It seems, however, that among Gentile "foreigners" the educated man often finds it harder to change, or to let his native-American son change, than does the plain peasant. He considers himself an intellectual. He is more conscious of his background than the uneducated man, perhaps more nationalistic in reference to the old country, and more attached to his patronymic which may be intimately linked with his earlier life in Poland or Hungary. This is apt to hold for some years after he comes here, and often he never gets over it. He is more romantic about the good aspects of the land of his birth and is likely to possess more talent for nostalgia than the unschooled ex-peasant who lived in extreme poverty in Europe and now works in a mine or steel mill in Pennsylvania or Illinois. Also, the intellectual immigrant may become a leader in some "foreign" section, editor of a foreign-language paper, or officer of an immigrant fraternal society or cultural club, and it would not do for him to alter his name.

Sometimes even if he is disposed to simplify it the intellectual immigrant refrains because his relatives in Europe would be distressed. This is particularly so if he belongs to a distinguished family whose name has historical significance. When my friend Stojan Pribičević, son of a great political leader in the early years of Yugoslavia, came to this country in the mid-1930's, he made a bid for some sort of pronunciation by spelling his name Stoyan Pribichevich. He worked in a Cleveland factory for a while where the foreman called him Pepperbitch. Eventually he began to write in English and move toward his present position on the editorial staff of *Fortune* magazine, and to lecture before clubs, forums, and college audiences. Then, he says, "the fun began." The best that most platform chairmen could do by way of introducing him was Mr. P-b-v-v-ich, "with the accent on the *b*." In literary and intellectual circles in New York most of the people he met were intrigued by his name and did their best to master it. "If they get the pronunciation right off," he told me, "they never forget it; if not, they never get it at all." Finally, his lecture agent laid down the law: he must change his name. Stoyan did not believe in radical alteration "particularly if a Balkanite thus became a pseudo-Scotchman," but he did not object to simplification. He knew, however, that his family in Serbia would suffer if he did anything to his. So for a while he turned his first name, Stoyan, into his surname for writing and lecturing purposes, retaining Pribichevich for all others. This was acceptable to his relatives abroad, where many writers take pen names. But lately—1941-42—I notice that on *Fortune's* masthead his name appears as Stoyan Pribichevich.

This sort of thing has its ups and downs, which depend on the person's inner processes and on exterior influences —for instance, such as the events in Yugoslavia during 1941-42 which tend to make many people prouder of their Yugoslav names than they were before.

Shame-Impelled and Secret Changing

His opinion was that there was a strange kind of magic bias which good or bad names, as he called them, irresistibly impressed upon our characters and conduct. . . . How many Caesars and Pompeys, he would say, by mere inspiration of the names, have been rendered worthy of them? And how many, he would add, are there who might have done exceeding well in the world, had not their characters and spirits been totally depressed and Nicodemus'd into nothing?

STERNE, *Tristram Shandy*, Bk. i, ch. 19

TOWARD MEDIOCRITY—WITH EXCEPTIONS

THE Polish Americans who spoke up in the meeting indicated the "storms" and doubts which disturb many people when they decide to rename themselves. None of their statements, however, delved into the feeling of shame and inferiority which drives great numbers of the younger immigrants and many more immigrants' American-born sons and daughters to modify their "foreign" names, usually by translation or transliteration into English cognomens, regardless of the pain such a step causes the parents. Nor did any of them touch on the subtle corrosion of personality many bring upon themselves by Anglicizing or otherwise changing their names.

O. E. Rölvaag has a character in his novel *Pure Gold*, a second-generation girl, Hazel Knapp, whose surname was shortened from Knapperud. She felt it an unbearable humiliation to have a grotesque Norwegian name and feared "real Americans" would think she was a recently arrived foreigner. This had an unfortunate effect on her as a person. In other novels and short stories dealing with immigrants and the second generation which were published during the 1930's, notably John Fante's and Guido D'Agostino's, similar characters have appeared; and before me is a heap of letters and memoranda on this subject—most of them marked "Confidential."

Some of this material—such as the two stories immediately following this chapter—I feel free to tell in disguise. The stories which I am not allowed to tell of shame-motivated, inorganic name-changing, usually accompanied by secrecy and fear, concern people of Slavic, Near Eastern, Italian and Hungarian descent. I don't know how

59

many such people there are; my impression is that their number is not negligible and that they stem from many new-immigrant groups.

They have got rid of their badges of alienism and become "Americans," but they are not at ease. In secretly discarding their "foreign" labels, in trying to ignore their problem, they have buried a good part of their chance for the sense of continuity apparently necessary to a well-rounded-out character. They are severed from what are normally the most vital influences in one's life, and the result—*with many exceptions,* let me emphasize—is hollowness and mediocrity. They pretend to be something they are not. Behind their fronts and new handles they are still Hunkies, Litvaks, Kikes, or Wops, as they sometimes admit to themselves, adding: when will I be discovered and exposed?

I must make it clear that this does not appear to be true of those who, by translation or transliteration, Anglicize their names openly as a matter of convenience, with some practical motive such as their business or profession, and who remain in the same community, continuing to mingle with people who knew them before the alteration. Here too, however, the change is not strictly organic. Some of them are often reminded that their name used to be Wawrzyniak or Kapcsos or Juodzinkas or Katchadourian or Tanaskovich, which makes them a little uncomfortable, but they take it in their stride, joke about it, and by-and-by gain acceptance for their new names.

Some have difficulty integrating their new names into their personalities. They cannot forget their old ones. In a West Coast city, in 1940, a businessman changed from Elmer Werkenheimer to Elmer Homer. He sent out announcements to that effect. Two months later he received a letter from one of his business friends who addressed him as "Mr. Elmer Werkenheimer." At the bottom of his reply

Mr. Homer put a P.S.: "May I recall to your mind that I changed my name to Elmer Homer? Please do not write to me under my old name any longer." The friend came back with a profuse apology: hereafter he would remember and address him by his new name. Mr. Homer acknowledged the apology, calling it unnecessary, and signed himself "Homer Werkenheimer."

Such cases, too, are numerous; but they are nothing to worry about.

Nor is there anything to bother about in instances where people openly and matter-of-factly lop a syllable or two off their "foreign" names or who openly change them in any other way—like the Mreches family who late in 1939 figured in New York newspapers. After long hesitation, they decided that the name was too much of a drawback. Mr. Mreches said no one could remember it, which lost him business. His nineteen-year-old son, a college student, thought he had received lower marks because his instructors, uncertain about its pronunciation, did not call on him. And Mrs. Mreches claimed that acquaintances "found it impossible to invite me to social functions because they so easily forgot the proper spelling and hesitated to embarrass me by misspelling it," and her social life was "ruined." So the Mrecheses changed to Marshall.

The Marshalls are probably all right now.

A moment ago I stressed the words *"with many exceptions"* in connection with the ill effect of secret, shamed name-changing and "passing." The exceptions are interesting. I know of the daughter of Jewish immigrants from Poland who, she assures me, succeeded in discarding not only her Jewish name but her personality and in taking on a new one. She knew what she wanted, went about putting herself over in a most determined way, and is apparently getting away with it. I have never met her; this information is taken from a letter she wrote me. She has a

Gentile husband, who is a prominent man. He knows she "was Jewish once," but nobody else does among the people "in our circle." She says that "everything is all right" and suggests that I "advise other girls to cease being Jewesses if they do not look Jewish." But I doubt if she is completely at ease within herself. Why should she write to me on hearing that I was interested in such matters?

A FAMILY OF "GREEKS" NAMED HICKS

THE parents came to the United States from Greece in the early 1900's and settled in a city in Ohio. Their name was highly honored in Greece and not very difficult to spell or pronounce in America. But it was a constant source of embarrassment to their American-born children because in that town, "for some unknown reason," to quote my informant, " 'Greek' is equivalent to 'Nigger' in the South." Things began to come to a head five or six years before Greece's heroic stand against the Axis in 1940-41, which led many old-stock or plain Americans to take a fresh look at the "Greeks" in their midst. Although both the father and the mother were educated and conversant with Hellenic virtues, they were unable to combat the sense of shame which often seized the young people because of their ancestry. The children even refused to be seen in the streets with their parents.

When he was sixteen, the oldest boy attempted suicide; then he ran away and was picked up in Kansas, claiming his name was Brown. The family went through increasingly frequent explosions; the situation developed into a kind of family psychosis. The climax came when the oldest daughter secretly married, largely as it turned out because she thereby became Mrs. Hicks. The marriage was on the rocks within two months, but before it broke up her younger brother assumed the name of Hicks. "There was hell to pay," says my correspondent, who watched the whole pathetic drama at close range; and in desperation the parents finally gave up the struggle and their name.

They all became Hicks.

But this solved nothing. The family was obliged to do

much explaining, which made everybody all the more aware they were "Greeks." There were nastier scenes at home than before. The situation became impossible. The children forced the parents to sell out and they all moved to Texas, where they have been in poor economic circumstances ever since.

The parents, now past middle age, are a tragic couple. In their own minds, "Hicks" does not fit them. They look "foreign"; they speak fairly good English, but with an accent. Two of the children still live at home, and they yell at them to pronounce this or that word so-and-so, but the old people cannot get rid of their accent—they spoke only Greek till their mid-twenties. Native Texans know they are "some kind of foreigners," which is worse than if they were just plain "Greeks." The prejudice against "foreigners" and "aliens," particularly strong in that part of Texas, has made it difficult for the father to get a new start in his business.

The children, my informant assures me, are "not fundamentally unintelligent" but are "so distorted now by this whole business that they can't see what it is doing to their father and mother and to themselves." They allow only "HICKS" on the mailbox in the hallway; and the parents, not daring to tell their relatives about the name-change, rent a post-office box for mail from the old country.

When the Greeks gave the good account of themselves against Mussolini which is now history, new difficulties arose in the "Hickses'" home. The parents, especially the old man, became extremely excited. He wanted to broadcast his ancestry. The half-dozen other Greek immigrants in town started a Greek War Relief organization and "Mr. Hicks" deeply desired to tell them he came from Corinth and wished to join them. But the younger "Hickses" put up a strong opposition. "There were terrific arguments," and at the end the old man gave in.

It was his ultimate defeat.

My correspondent suspects that during the Italo-Greek war the young people at moments "came close to being proud of being 'Greeks,' but they could not straighten themselves out; their whole history was against any such thing. When Germany finally conquered Greece, they were relieved it was all over. . . ."

ALIAS JULIA DRINKWATER

ONE day in the late 1930's an attractive young woman, Julia Drinkwater, applied for the position of secretary to a doctor in Newark, New Jersey, a friend of mine, who has since told me about her.

She got the job.

She had a marked if somewhat unconvincing English accent and pronounced her name Drink'atter—"like the poet, you know." It gradually developed that she was of old-stock Yankee parentage, born in Brookline, Massachusetts, but that she had been brought up and educated in England where her widowed father represented an American firm. After his death, four years before, her grandmother in Brookline invited her to return to the United States. Her circumstances obliged her to accept, for her father had left her very little. But she did not get along with her grandmother ("that is a long story, Doctor"), and she went to New York for secretarial training. She now lived in Manhattan; most of her friends were there; but she found it pleasant to work in New Jersey.

To the doctor, who is very acute about people, she did not ring entirely true. Not only was her English accent inconsistent, but in her speech seemed to be echoes of what had once passed for English in Brownsville, the great Jewish section in Brooklyn, near which he had lived for some years. He was busy and tried not to wonder about her. What difference did it make what she really was? She was efficient. He didn't think he would keep her very long anyhow; she was good-looking and somebody was bound to marry her soon. But he could not help asking her an occasional question. And once or twice she volunteered information about herself. In an amused, offhand tone, she told him that among her ancestors were a Colonial governor and an aide-de-camp to George Washington whom she named. It occurred to the doctor that he had never heard of an American family named Drinkwater. She hesitated a moment, then replied that during the Revolutionary War her paternal ancestors had been Tories who had run off to Canada. She looked a little embarrassed and continued that she was "really a little Canadian"; her father's father had come down to Boston from Nova Scotia in the '80s.

One evening she telephoned the doctor at his home. Her grandmother had died and she would have to go to Brookline for two or three days. Although her story hung together, the doctor now suddenly disbelieved her completely. A phrase she used sounded clearly Jewish-Brooklynese. Also some years before he had developed a near-complex against employees' using dead grandmothers to get away for ball games and dates. But she had filled her job well for nine months; so, more curious than distrustful, he said, "I'm very sorry, Julia. I realize you and your grandmother did not click any too well, but just as a gesture of my regard for you I'd like to wire flowers. Where will the services be held?"

This flustered Julia. She said it was terribly nice of him, but she didn't know the address. Her English accent cracked on the word "address."

The doctor urged her to put in a long-distance call and find out. Miss Drinkwater said she would try. "Then call me again and tell me," said the doctor.

Julia said she would, but didn't.

She turned up two days later, and with almost no trace of an English accent told the doctor she needed his advice; it was a long story. She began by saying that her real name was not Drink'atter but Robinovitz. Her people came from Russia. Garment workers. She was a Hunter College graduate. She had hated being Jewish and "foreign." She had loathed the sound of "Robinovitz," especially with her first name. Cora Robinovitz! She did not "look Jewish." She was not Jewish, whatever that meant apart from having parents who regarded themselves as Jews, so why be a Jew? Why be called Cora Robinovitz? In 1936 she changed her name first to Julia Warner, then to Julia Drinkwater. She took her secretarial course under that name.

This was her third position. After becoming Drinkwater, she felt "quite English." She read English authors, subscribed to the weekly edition of the London *Times*, and planned to go to England as soon as possible. But she had to earn a living, and she could not save anything because she had to have a nice apartment and good clothes. She preferred to work in New Jersey, where some of the fine people she knew in New York were not likely to come upon her sitting at a typewriter.

She liked being English, she said, but also wanted to be an American; so she built up the story she had told him. Most of the time it was quite real to her. She *felt* both American and English. She had a number of old-stock American friends who never questioned her origin and her life in England. She had spent a lot of time practicing an English accent. Even now she saw at least twice every Broadway play or movie with English characters. It was a strain, of course, to be something one really wasn't— "wasn't in a sense, that is"—but it was worth it to be Julia Drinkwater—"and I really am Julia Drinkwater, Doctor—*really*!" Here she lapsed into her pseudo-English accent.

Smiling, the doctor asked why her grandmother in Brookline had had to die all of a sudden.

Julia's face lightened a moment; she hesitated, then

said, "Because I am in a mess. And from here on I shall probably sound like a gal out of *True Stories*. My special friends are a family I have known for a couple of years. They are awfully nice, all of them, and *really* real Americans. They go all the way back to the *Mayflower*, although they don't give a hoot about it—which is wonderful. I wish I were that way. Since I've known them, I have tried to appear casual about my own fictional background. I can see this seems really funny to you, Doctor," she said when he smiled. He noticed that "really" was now in the American, now in the English intonation.

"Anyhow," Cora Robinovitz, alias Julia Drinkwater, continued, "I have been seeing these people in New York and week-ends at their place in Montauk. One of the girls, Jane, and I are particularly good friends. Her brother Jack is in Annapolis, and we three have fun together. Dances; theater. Jane is amused by the way my English-English speech, as she calls it, is being mixed up with American, and we laugh over it.

"Here comes the important part. Jack's best friend Bill is another midshipman who has been going out with us. I have been to Annapolis twice, and we had a marvelous time. But I'll tell you only the barest facts. Bill and I fell in love with each other. He is from upstate New York, part Swedish, part German, and the rest American: but none of this matters to him and it doesn't to me; I mean he is really all American. He is wonderful, and he thinks I am.

"And I *am* all right, too; I *know* I am. Only, when I'm alone in my apartment, and even here in the office, I have been wondering if it would matter to him if he knew that in a sense I am not really Julia Drink'atter, that I have never been in England, and that I am Jewish—although, so far as I am concerned, I am not *really*. It is certain to matter if he finds out I have been lying to him, especially about being Jewish—although I want to say again I am not Jewish, not *really*, so far as I am concerned.

"But in a way I *am* a fake; at least everybody would agree I am—Jane and Jack, I am afraid, and their mother who is a darling, and their friends; and I wouldn't blame them. And how would Bill react? He is wonderfully insane about me. But ——

"Bill and Jack are being commissioned next month. In July, Jack is going to marry an awfully sweet girl, whose grandfather was a naval officer in the Spanish-American War and whose mother has a house on Shelter Island, and another at Coronado in California; and Bill wants to marry me at the same time. Bill is going to be Jack's best man and he wants Jack to be his. When I called you night before last, I had just received a wire from him: he was coming to New York the next day and had to see me alone.

"I don't want—I can't tell you, Doctor, what happened yesterday. This sounds melodramatic or something, but it's so. I had intended to tell Bill everything, but I didn't. I couldn't. He's so grand. Then, when he left me last night, I nearly went mad. What could I do? I said I would let him know in a week; a week from yesterday. I want to marry him. . . . I decided to talk to you, Doctor. I've felt before you were suspicious. When you offered to send flowers to my grandmother's funeral, I was sure ——"

The doctor asked the young lady about her Jewish family. Her mother was dead. Her father lived with her married sister in the Bronx. Her brother was still in Brownsville, a plumber. She had seen them last three years ago. She didn't like any of them.

"What can I do, Doctor?"

He didn't know what to say. He remarked he wanted to think it over. He would talk to her again.

The next two days he was extremely busy and had no

opportunity to speak with his secretary except about professional matters and to ask her once or twice how she was. She said in a remote voice that she was all right. She evidently wasn't. The doctor still didn't know how to advise her. On Saturday he suggested she come to his house Monday evening. He said they had better tell his wife about it; she had straightened out a number of love crinkles.

On Monday Julia neither turned up at the office nor telephoned.

After three days the doctor tried in vain to communicate with her. Her telephone was disconnected. A wire came back. She had left the apartment and, as he discovered later, nearly all her belongings, which included some Early American glass. By calling most of the plumber Robinovitzes in Brooklyn, he got in touch with her brother who said indifferently that he hadn't seen his sister Cora for three or four years.

The doctor has had no word of her since. He is sure the last story she told him is true, and that she did not marry Bill, but simply vanished.

WHAT IS A NAME?

THE "Hicks" and "Drinkwater" instances are of course extreme. But many people are unfavorably affected by a new name even if they take it openly, sensibly, for the sake of practical convenience. Some seem to hang on the verge of psychological disaster for the rest of their lives.

How to explain this?

A name is a word which in itself has next to no meaning. It is merely a tag. It means almost no more than the word "the," which is technically, grammarians tell me, a deictic particle. In other words, "the" is a pointer-outer, which is what a name is. Say "the" a dozen times and see how much meaning it has. Now say "the man" and you've got something. Add "short" and "fat" and the meaning expands while its application narrows. Now add "semi-bald" and there is more meaning within a still narrower range; then "stubborn." You begin to get warm, and I suspect who the short, fat, semi-bald, stubborn man is; but I may be wrong, for I know more than one. Now try "Jenkins." Say it a dozen times. To some it may connote English or American middle or lower class; to most, nothing whatever, or nothing they want to bother with, if they say it a hundred times. It is very much like "the," which simply separates words. A name simply separates one man from the rest, saying *This* is the man I am talking about." It doesn't tell much about him. Most Smiths are not smiths; few Grays are gray or Blacks black. But while a name as such has no intrinsic meaning, what little special meaning it may have for some people is almost always limited by linguistic, national, historical or antiquated class connotations. It also may acquire special meanings by association for a particular person or group. But for most of the human race it is merely a pointer, like an outstretched index finger. Like "the," it communicates only direction.

To its possessor, however, as already suggested, a name may have loads of meaning, although some—perhaps most —of it is strictly private and outside the realm of verbal communication, except for such proud but poetically vague statements as that of a character in Scott's *Rob Roy* who exclaims, "My foot is on my native heath, and my name is MacGregor!" or Gladstone's: "My name may have buoyancy enough to float upon the sea of time."

Lots of people try in vain to conceal their gratified enjoyment at seeing their names in print. Indeed, to some people their names are all important. As with Kobotchnik and the Randolph I know, or one or two of the Polish Americans I have quoted, their names are themselves— there is a profound identification.

The feeling which children manifest about their names is illuminating. We teach them to say, "My name is Paul; what's yours?" But what they actually do say is, "I'm Paul; who are you?" If both have the same name there is bewilderment or disbelief: "How can he be Paul? I'm Paul!" Such a complete identification heightens the traumatic effect of teasing upon youngsters named Algernon, say, or Claude or Percy. I have heard of a young man whose mother bestowed on him the name of Sylvan. Tired of being called Sylvia in school, he managed to slide imperceptibly into "Sylvan J. Greenfield," then to "S. Jerome Greenfield." Now everybody, even his mother, calls him simply "Jerry," which somehow suits him perfectly.

It might not be a bad idea to ask boys and girls when they begin to grow up if they would like to change their names. Their decision should be free, however, of any outside pressure, and should be scrupulously observed. This would be nothing new. The Chinese have the custom of giving children temporary or "milk" names, then letting them choose their own first names later.

Taking a man's name away from him may permanently harm his personality or even destroy it. It is done for punishment in some penitentiaries where prisoners are given numbers, and its effect on some convicts is almost worse than incarceration itself. In the regions around Trieste, which were taken over by Italy after the First World War, all the Slovenian names (even on tombstones) were suddenly and forcibly Italianized by Mussolini back in the early 1920's, and I am informed that at least partly in consequence of this some Slovenians began to disintegrate almost visibly, not only as Slovenian nationalists who hated Mussolini and Italian rule but also within themselves as human beings. I assume that if Hitler rules Europe for any considerable time the same process will be observable in Alsace-Lorraine where in the spring of 1941 the Nazis ordered all inhabitants with French names to give them up for German ones. Somehow it seems that being deprived of their "real" names is the final defeat for a lot of people.

Disaster may occur, as I say, even where persons change their names of their own presumably free will for obviously good reasons. Mental decision and the immediate, practical reasons often go contrary to what Tacitus had in mind, I think, when he mentioned the "superstition of a name." Kobotchnik was miserable as Cabot. My guess is that during the thirty-seven years as Cabot he was not quite the man he might have been if his wife had allowed him to remain Kobotchnik. But, of course, had his character been stronger (or different) to begin with, he would not have let her get away with it.

Why name-changing should be harmful I can't say exactly, but it has come up again and again during my inquiries over the last three years. It is subtle, remote, primitive. It lies below the level of reason. The reaction of children to names—even the dog Nurmi's response to "Buster"—can be examined with profit. A young man once told me of the hours he spent in childhood wondering why he was himself—was John—instead of someone else.

To many people the problem of their own identity is inextricably concerned with that of finding their natural place, their creative or productive niche in the world of human beings. The claims of the ego are strong; no less so are those of society; and the civilization process is after all a seeking of the balance-point between the two extremes. The identification of name with ego reaches backward beyond family and nationalism. It may be influenced by tribal memory, not of any actual details in primitive society but of the general feeling about the significance of one's name—a transmitted, formless, still-functioning residue. To a primitive man, anthropologists tell us (see Frazer's *The Golden Bough*), his name is very important. To this day, in some savage tribes a child is given a private name to be guarded in secrecy throughout his life. Known abroad, it constitutes a danger. As long as outsiders know only his public name he is safe from baleful magic; but with his secret name his enemy acquires power over him. This attitude is reflected in ancient religions. The name of the deity was to be uttered sparingly by the priests alone and then only among the initiate. In writing, a symbol or substitute was used. To say the name exposed the deity to his enemies and endangered the life of the utterer, unless he also was sacred. This feeling and practice survive among secret societies, including college fraternities with their concealed, unwritten mottoes.

In the savage atmosphere of the Europe of 1942 it is

widespread in underground movements. There, of course, passwords and secret names are thoroughly practical. But they are also a reversion to primitive superstition. Paradoxically, many people who go into underground work with secret names do so for the highest ideals of human progress, yet in the process many disintegrate as individuals and idealists, becoming more savage than civilized. I observed this in Yugoslavia during 1932-33 in some of the underground people working against the dictatorship of King Alexander, and I don't doubt that in the specific cases I have in mind much of their inner collapse was due to switching names at a time when their own cognomens had begun to acquire meaning for them. In conjunction with other more obvious factors in their new lives, the aliases stirred up a confusion not only of identification but of identity. They became two or more persons and thus actually no-person. It seems that under such circumstances only the most firmly civilized can maintain their integrity and escape a split personality and irresponsibility.

The same process has been observable for years in the American Communist party, which although legal has sometimes functioned here and there as an underground activity. Many of its members have secret names. I know at least one whose disintegration of character is partly due, I believe, to his three-year-long pseudonymity. In 1934 he was unquestionably an idealist; by 1937, after registering under his party name at many hotels and airplane depots, he could be described accurately only as a scoundrel. And I have data on others.

Of course the name factor in personal decline cannot be neatly isolated from others—such as the sudden and fantastic changes in the "party line" and the movement's idea that the end justifies the means. But I am satisfied that the use of secret names within the Communist party of the United States is partly the cause of some of the

human wreckage now strewn about in the American rad-
ical-intellectual world—although I am quite willing to
agree that the cause of the wreckage was not so much the
pseudonymity as the whole process of living in deceit.

The problem of name-changing goes as far and as deep
as all this. *Not with everybody,* to be sure. Nor, perhaps,
even with most people. A man may be so fortunate as to
take the intelligent world's attitude toward his name and
not care very much what it is, how it is spelled or
pronounced. The late Jake Falstaff, a columnist on the
Cleveland Press and author of a number of books, was
such a man. Once he was asked why he wrote under the
name of Falstaff, since his name was really Herman Fetzer.
He replied: "The decision was made after I had been
called Fetzlar, Fessler, Fetzgar, Fletcher, Feathers, Fitzer,
Fegster, Fespers and Feldspar. There is relieving novelty
in being called Flagstaff, Felstoff, Fogstaff and Fatstiff."
With many, however, the psychological fusion of their
names with their personal identity—as distinguished from
the rest of mankind—is well-nigh complete. And a lot of
people are not yet sufficiently integrated within themselves and with society to feel perfectly natural and easy
about what the course of living does to their names. This
goes, I believe, for nearly all immigrants and a majority
of their American-born children.

Generally speaking, the less the quantity and intensity
of emotion attached to or repelled by one's name, the
more organic will be whatever happens to it. And strength
of intellect does not keep one from getting into an emotional stew over one's name. Arthur Koestler, the Hungarian author of two remarkable books, *Darkness at Noon*
and *Scum of the Earth,* which have appeared in the United
States, is equipped with a strong—almost a tough, hard-
boiled—mind; yet, as he tells on page 249 of the latter
book, he could not keep himself from fretting over his

name after circumstances had made it necessary for him
to change it. To escape from the Gestapo in France,
Koestler had joined the French Foreign Legion and been
given the Swiss name of Dubert. Now and then he seemed
to get so used to it that when an acquaintance hailed him
one day by his old name "it sounded uncanny." But sometimes he felt so lost that he repeated to himself "half aloud
my name, the real one." This conveyed to him "a feeling
of complete irreality," taking him out of the plight in
which he found himself. One day he wrote in his diary:
"Had never known what importance one attached to one's
name, and what a queer, amputated feeling it is to lose it."

In his well-known book, *How to Make Friends and Influence People,* Dale Carnegie's "Rule 3" for success, especially in politics and business, is: "Remember that a man's
name is to him the sweetest and most important sound in
the English language." Even, I might add, if the name is
not English.

Dale Carnegie ascribes one of the greatest political suc-
cesses in modern history, that of Franklin D. Roosevelt,
to the realization that "one of the simplest, most obvious,
and most important ways of gaining good will is by re-
membering names and making people feel important."
He says that one of the first lessons an aspiring politician
must learn is: "To recall a voter's name is statesmanship.
To forget it is oblivion."

To Change or Not to Change

I would rather make my name than inherit it.

THACKERAY, *The Virginians,* Ch. 26

Giving a name, indeed, is a poetic art; all poetry, if we go to that with it, is but a giving of names.

CARLYLE, *Journal,* 18 May, 1832

Few men have grown unto greatness whose names are allied to ridicule.

M. F. TUPPER, *Proverbial Philosophy,* i. 1838

MANY HANG ONTO THEM—SOME FOR
DEAR LIFE

I MAY have given the impression that the proclivity to alter "foreign" surnames is much greater than it is. The telephone directories of Greater New York, Boston, Philadelphia, Chicago, Detroit, Cleveland, Pittsburgh and hundreds of lesser cities and towns contain vast numbers of old-country names in unaltered or but slightly modified forms. On a considerable proportion of phone-book pages, in fact, "foreign" names predominate—and it should be borne in mind that, owing to their economic circumstances or Old-World backwardness, most new-immigrant families have no telephones.

The daily press contains items like these in the July 15, 1941, *PM*:

Julian Kwiatkowski, 71, was arraigned on a charge of forging a check for $75. The complainant was Gregory Werberchowsky, owner of a bar and grill. . . .

Two firemen, William Buteau and Joseph Jelincke, fished Efrosinia Borovkova, 45, out of the water at Battery Park. She had become discouraged. She is a teacher in the Soviet Private School at 6 E. 87th St. Dr. Joseph Spiaggia treated her.

Hundreds of thousands of "foreign" patronymics are being retained in spite of the impatience of the English language, in spite of direct and indirect demands for alteration and in the face of personal and professional disadvantages. Millions of immigrants and native-American sons and daughters of foreign parents remain Mikolajczak, Kohulik, Wohlgemuth, Srb, Miklisich, Kotalik, Vaczy, Stofa, Kudirka, Bartolini, Kotakis, Vojvodich, Jezik, Giannacoulis, Zsilavecz, Kalmonek, Tomasko, Sedlacek, Usala,

81

Hecherblickner, Bavlsik, Kowbasniuk, Kikuchi, Sojka, Drozdik, and Vishnevetsky, although, so far as law is concerned, it would be the easiest thing in the world to change. In some states, one need not even go to court; one is free to take any name, any time as long as there is no fraudulent intent.

Above I list "Kikuchi." It is the name of a young *nisei* or second-generation Japanese American I know in California. In *From Many Lands* I called him "A Young American With a Japanese Face." In the spring of 1942, with everybody else of his race, he was evacuated from San Francisco as a matter of military necessity, but he is passionately American. For a time in college, back in the late 1930's, he would have liked to erase every trace of his Japanese background but in common with practically all the *nisei* he never entertained the idea of "Americanizing" his surname. With his Japanese face Charlie Kikuchi would have been an incongruity had he changed, say, to Kirkconnel or Kingdon. He has a strong sense of what is fitting, and an "American" name would have worsened the doldrums he was going through as Kikuchi. This applies largely to Chinese Americans, except that a good many of them are Li and Yung, which they can spell Lee and Young—common names both in China and in America.

The Caucasian new-immigrant groups, however, have no racial or facial deterrent, and yet perhaps a considerable majority of them have not changed their names, many of which are really twisters. Why?

People are not just stubborn, contrary and nationalistic; the deeply-rooted instinct which I have discussed insists on their old tags. In their minds many think it best to change, but they are caught in a helpless and hopeless inability to decide. Many others have more conscious but just as effective reasons for not changing. Nearly everywhere in the country, while a great many patronymics *are* being altered, there is an increasing determination not to

Anglicize names or to simplify them to the point of obscuring their origin. This is almost as true of native Americans of foreign derivation as of immigrants.

The attitude of a young Chicago friend of mine, John Switalski, is typical of many people with "foreign" names. John is a third-generation American of Polish and German descent who considers himself a Polish American. His name comes to him from his paternal grandfather, a refugee from Prussian Poland in the eighties. Early in the 1930's he spent two years in Poland. Many of the aspects of the country appealed to him and fostered a pride undiminished since by Hitler's easy conquest in 1939. Once he debated changing his name; now, when the suggestion is made, he replies that there are more Switalskis than Roosevelts in the United States. Something like forty families live in Chicago alone and about thirty each in Buffalo and Detroit. In 1940 he and his wife, also of Polish descent, christened their first child Barbara Jadwiga after two famous Polish queens. They call her Basia, the name of one of Sienkiewicz's most delightful feminine characters. The John Switalskis mingle with people of all backgrounds. Although slightly on the defensive occasionally, they are not belligerent in their attitude. They can take whatever unpleasantness arises over the name which they consider logically theirs. John believes that discrimination against names like his will vanish as conditions in the United States gradually improve, with some luck, under the dynamic mass-will of the American people functioning within the country's democratic political setup, which he believes to be a result of centuries of thinking and fighting by people of various backgrounds, including a couple of generals named Pulaski and Kosciuszko. His defensiveness, indicated by the importance to him of his name, also comes out in emphasizing (but not exaggerating) the role of Poles in the inception and development of the United States.

Striking is the case of a Sergeant Hitler of the United States Army which was reported in the press in May, 1941. He was ribbed about his name and advised to change it. But he declared, "Let the other guy change it!" Another Hitler who is a soldier in the American Army (and, incidentally, a Jew) said: "It's my name and I have a perfect right to use it. But Adolf hasn't. His name is Schicklgruber."

This attitude toward "foreign" names has been clearly in the ascendancy since the middle 1930's in most new-immigrant groups. It rose with the extensive and favorable newspaper publicity received in the United States by Poland, Czechoslovakia, Finland, Yugoslavia, Sweden and other "old countries" in consequence of international developments. The publicity endowed many Americans of older stocks with a respect for the new strains; which, in turn, brought on a lessening of the latter's sense of inferiority over being "foreigners." To some of the new Americans it even occurred, off and on, that being of Czech or Finnish descent and being named Hrybasek or Aaltonen was a subtle something in their favor.

A number of books which were widely read during the late 1920's and 1930's both by old-stock and by new-immigrant groups had an influence in breaking down the feeling of shame in American-born children of immigrants and replacing it with a positive attitude. Marquis Childs's volume on the democratic "middle way" in Sweden had a salutary effect on Swedish Americans, even on those who only heard it discussed. One of its results was to send many native Americans vaguely troubled about being "dumb Swedes" or "squareheads" to Sweden, whence most returned with a proud consciousness of their background. Marie Sandoz's popular *Old Jules*, the story of her Swiss pioneer father in Nebraska, evoked a respect for the new elements generally, which in turn gave them more self-assurance. This was also true, of course, of Willa Cather's novel, *My Ántonia,* dealing with Czech pioneers in Nebraska, and of O. E. Rölvaag's Norwegian saga. Eve Curie's biography of her mother had an inestimable value for Polish Americans. Franz Werfel's epic *The Forty Days of Musa Dagh* strongly influenced native Americans of Armenian parentage, and may be partly responsible for the following editorial which appeared in the October 9, 1940, *The Armenian Mirror-Spectator,* an English-language weekly published in New York which circulates largely among the second generation:

To change or not to change, that is the question. Whether 'tis nobler to stick, through thick or thin, to the four or five syllable names of one's ancestors, or by one rebellious act end them.

The average immigrant Armenian is torn between loyalty to his forebears and the necessity of having a fairly pronounceable name. But to change is even today tantamount to treason in the estimation of one's countrymen. On the other hand, life becomes exasperating when a person has to make every fellow citizen of other backgrounds understand that his name is, for instance, Jebidelikian.

Armenian names fall into three classes: (1) pure Armenian names, satisfactory from the point of euphony, (2) pure Armenian names, long and not suitable for the Anglo-Saxon tongue, (3) Turkish names. Any attempt to change names that fall in the first category betrays mental instability or some other psychological aberration. Those that fall in the second category could often be shortened with satisfactory results. The only names that justify a major operation are those of the last category. For even the "patriots" cannot convince us that there is anything sacred in remaining attached to a name which represents a negation of one's ancestral identity. The mere appendage of an *ian* is the only redeeming feature of such names.

As for the growing custom of assuming high-falutin Anglo-Saxon names, we can simply say that it is the poorest though easiest way out of the situation. Names serve to identify a person along with his background, and therefore, unless one has reasons to hide that background, he has little excuse to bedeck himself with feathers belonging to other birds.

I quote it in full because it is typical of statements that have been appearing since 1938 in many foreign-language newspapers and English-language second-generation journals, which are being started in many parts of the country. I have before me similar clippings from *Nowy Swiat* (Polish: New York), *Szabadzag* (Hungarian: Cleveland), *The American Slav* (Pittsburgh), *The Hellenic Spectator* (Washington), and *Opinion* (Jewish: New York).

I have said that Jews had no strong cognominal tradition. Still, in its September, 1939, issue, *Opinion* published an editorial about a Jewish family named Einstein who changed to Easton for two reasons: first, "Einstein is distinctly German and Semitic"; second, the change would "greatly enlarge" the opportunities for advancement of two sons attending the Naval and Military academies. "The delightful thing about the abandonment of the name Einstein," said the editorial, "is that it marks the rejection of one of the best known and most honored names on earth." As for the reason, apparently endorsed by the authorities at Annapolis and West Point, that a Jewish name would handicap the young men in the naval and military services, "what of Commodore Urich P. Levy and Admiral Joseph Strauss and Captain Adolph Marix? We would fain convey to the heads of the Academies . . . that passion for advancement at the cost of self-respect is not a merit but a disease. . . . Incidentally, it may be observed that Albert Einstein had to change his country but his name remains unchanged. Hitler's Reich rejected him. But our country will celebrate the day . . . which gives Albert Einstein (not Arthur Easton) to American citizenship."

But of course this sort of reasoning, among Jews and Gentiles, is nothing new. The January, 1930, *American*

Legion Monthly published an article, "Why I Would Not Change My Name," by Elias Tobenkin, a Russian-Jewish immigrant who became a well-known American journalist and served during the First World War as an official propagandist with the Committee on Public Information, specializing in writing about the growth of democratic civilization in the United States. I quote by special permission:

I am typical . . . of . . . American citizens of European birth to whom their "foreign name" . . . has become a problem and a grief. In despair many have changed their names. [Mr. Tobenkin has here indirect reference to the violent alien-baiting tendencies of the 1920's.]

Dismay was my first reaction when I was told it was not inconceivable that my foreign name might prove a serious handicap to my future as an American. The one who told me this was a sincere man, of statesmanlike caliber, the editor-in-chief of one of the best-known magazines in the country. . . . He had printed two or three of my stories. He now had [a new] assignment for me . . . a series of six articles . . . a year's work. . . . Half a dozen writers, the editor informed me with evident satisfaction, had been considered for the enterprise and I was unanimously voted as the one best fitted for the job. A thrill ran through me. It was followed by an anticlimax.

Would I assume an American name for the series, the editor suggested. The management of the magazine felt, he explained, that the effect of the articles might be considerably lessened if they appeared under a name that was not native to the country.

I had behind me a newspaper experience of seven years and anonymous writing was not new to me. As a reporter my work had not always been signed and as an editorial writer [on the *Chicago Tribune*] I of course had to merge myself with the individuality of the paper. Nevertheless, to give an entire year to the study of a subject, to earn a national reputation in the writing of it, and to bestow this reputation on a fictitious name—I was incapable of such a sacrifice. When, after some speechless moments, I recovered the use of my voice, I so told the editor.

Back again at my desk . . . , I ruminated the matter. My name, which for 25 years or longer had been one with my physical and mental self, had suddenly become something detachable. Like the hat on one's head or the links on one's cuffs, it could be taken off, changed or thrown away. For the first time in my life I was holding my name up to the light, as it were, inspecting and examining it. Whence came it? What did it signify? Why had I been so obstinate in my refusal to part with it and take on a more pleasing Anglo-Saxon name— the word "Nordic" had then not yet come into vogue.

Just before falling asleep that night my thoughts winged off to the old world, to the village by the River Niemen in Russia where I was born. . . . One [memory] stood out above all others. It was the day I was admitted to the intermediary school in the capital of our province.

Children of the nobility, of merchants and officials alone were sent there. I also wanted to go there and my parents arranged with a distant relative in the capital to board me. I enrolled and took the examination. On a Thursday the result would be made known. Early in the morning carriages began to drive up in front of the school. At 11 the reading of the names of those who were admitted began. The lucky ones were escorted from the auditorium amid suppressed excitement and congratulations.

My name was read. I stepped up to the platform and was given a card of admission. As I retraced my steps, eyes were leveled upon me, as they had been upon the other successful applicants, curious to see what family circle would close about me. There was no one waiting for me and I walked out of the hall uncongratulated and alone.

But I was not alone. My name was with me. All the way to my lodgings I kept repeating to myself my name and the grade to which I was admitted as they had been read off by the school official. I was the only one from the village by the Niemen who made the school at the capital. It was as if my name had been written in a book with golden covers.

However, for months after my conversation with the editor

I was uneasy and in doubt. Had I acted rightly in clinging to my Old World name? And it was a problem millions . . . had to face.

Now as long as the retention or modification of their foreign name was merely a question of convenience in the daily intercourse with their American neighbors, the changing of names by immigrants from Eastern and Southern Europe had, on the whole, proceeded at a conservative pace, much the same as the changing or modifying of names by older generations of immigrants. It was only when the passions let loose by the World War and post-war prejudices began making names of other than Anglo-Saxon or Nordic character a taunt and a burden that these immigrants, and more especially those American born and bred, began [during the 1920's] divesting themselves of such names wholesale.

They chose their new names from their American histories and school texts, their only guide being to see that the first letter of their altered or new name corresponded with the name they were discarding. Thus there is a clan of Bradfords today whose name less than half a dozen years ago was Balabanoff; of Garfields whose name had been Golovenchik. A former Walliewica has become Wells; Linetzky has become Lawton; Borochoff has become Brooks; Michalsky has become Millford; Simkhovich has become Shepherd. . . .

Personally, I will not say that I never had occasion to regret not having changed my name to one that would permit me to lose myself readily in the community in which I lived. There is milk of human kindness in every person. But, whether men or children, human beings in the aggregate sometimes become merciless. There is something about the anonymity of a crowd which permits men in bulk to commit deeds of discrimination and cruelty that they would not do singly.

It is not for myself, however, that I regret most my not having changed my name, but for my little son. I recall days and days, some years ago, when he would come home from school or play with his little brow wrinkled. After several unsuccessful attempts I finally overcame his reticence. What was troubling him? I demanded.

"O," he said, "I wish we had an American name like others."

And then he added: "Teacher keeps talking about a Russian named Lenintrotsky, who is a good-for-nothing and a trouble-maker. Every time she mentions his name the kids in the class look at me as if I were a relation of his or something. Some of them tease me about it."

He was too young to be told that there was a stage in human history when the ancestors of the children who were now teasing him had themselves been teased about their origin. They had been called Barbarians by Roman soldiers and patrician Roman schoolmasters pronounced their Saxon and other Northern names with disdain.

He was too young to be told that. But I did tell him of Rudolph Valentino, whom he saw on the screen, and whom America had taken into her affections despite the fact that his name had a South European ending. I mentioned Rach-maninoff, whose Slav name did not make his music less sweet. I told him of Steinmetz and Pupin and Michelson, wizards of electricity, physics and astronomy, whose names and origins had been no bar to their passing on to the immortal regions of genius.

As simply as I could I explained that for me to change my name for gain of ease, to escape occasional prejudice or annoy-ance, would be an insult to the country which gave me birth, to my ancestors, dead and living, to their past with its heritage and achievements.

Most of all it would be an insult to the country that has adopted me and now calls me her own. America would lose her magic, would become no different from any other country, if it were said of her with truth that she is no longer the protagonist of fair play and equality for all, and that an en-trance card, in the shape of a changed name and an obliter-ated past, is required in order freely to enjoy the blessings of citizenship under her skies.

These statements are part of the American battle of names—of the psychological civil war. Mostly they are just blind instinct or feeling; some of it, as I have sug-gested, harking back to man's primitive experience or ris-ing from the deep-seated drive for personal identity within the whole of humanity, and the problem of what Professor Gissing called "the consciousness of kind." Such statements—referring not so much to Mr. Tobenkin's as to the others—erupt under irritation. They document the spasmodic sense of insecurity of new-immigrant groups and individuals. If you study them closely, however, and discuss them amicably with those who write them, you discover that at bottom they are trying to get at something like this:

"Don't let's take on tags by which we don't come naturally. Don't let's pretend to be something we are not. Let's be ourselves. So we did come from Hungary; so our parents are emigrants from Armenia, Poland, Finland, Greece, the Carpathians—what's wrong with that? Don't let's try to leap chasms; few of us can make it. Don't let us resort to escapes, evasions, faking. Let's proceed from *where* we are, *as* we are. Fact of the matter is, we can't honestly and intelligently do anything else."

This attitude strikes me as basically sound.

In it, however, are implications not easy to take for many old-line Americans who also are on the defensive—against the new strains—or whose thinking and feeling still swing confidently around old New England or Southern assumptions. In spite of the presence here of about 50,000,000 new-immigrant people, not a few old-stock Americans go on believing they are on the inside track of a pattern of civilization and culture which was fixed long ago, once and for all. Their most emphatic representative is editor of the magazine issued by a great patriotic organization which publishes nothing about anything which has happened less than fifty years ago.

But the attitude I have called sound does not deny that in a very real sense the matrix of the civilization of the United States is largely Anglo-Saxon. Nor does it cast any reflection whatever on the achievements of the Anglo-Saxon stock. It simply suggests that the human composition of the country as it now stands is not preponderantly Anglo-Saxon, but is rather a broad extension of all Europe and, in smaller proportion, of other continents.

This attitude holds that it is foolish for any Americans, and particularly for old-stock strains in leadership, to assume that their country is not such a human extension of a large part of the world; for in that fact lies one of its chief glories and sources of strength. Any pressure upon non-Anglo-Saxon elements to Anglicize themselves beyond the minimum demands of English speech, or to hide behind Anglo-Saxon labels contradicts reality, to say the least.

Complicated as is the question of names, I believe it is but the clearest manifestation of immense and as yet barely recognized cultural stirrings in the United States. The new strains, as I have said, are becoming aware that the United States includes people from all over the world. They do not bring this up, however, merely to say in the next breath that their mother country, Poland or Slovenia, is a place with such-and-such virtues. They feel, rather, that the American people as a whole ought to get away from the hangovers of all parts of the Old World as it was when they or their forebears left it, and create here a really New World in which some of the good things of the Old—of Albania, Slovenia, Bohemia, Germany, China and the Ukraine no less than of England, Ireland, Wales and Scotland—will be fused into a new culture.

This stirring, as I call it, is rather new and scarcely perceptible in the great maze of group and individual self-consciousness. In some new-immigrant elements it probably does not exist at all; in others it is hardly more than a sporadic instinctual aspiration. But it has power. And for a while I think it will find expression mostly in resisting the old demand and desire for Anglicization of "foreign" names. It will not be a very intelligent expression. It will be mixed up with the primitive hangover concerning names. To the hasty and undiscerning it will appear irrelevant or even "un-American." But it will be important.

The power of this feeling is such that thousands of individuals are suddenly eager to recover their "foreign" names. In Gary, Indiana, I have a friend, Louis Christopher, who regrets having given up his original Serbian name, Kristoforovich; but taking it back now would involve too many business complications. In Seattle I know an ex-State Senator of Washington who goes by the name of Miller and who in 1938 began to write his old Ukrainian name alongside it in parentheses: (Mlinyak). In the spring of 1942, on the Pacific Coast, I met a man who goes under the name of Mitchell. He told me he might change back to his original Serbian name of Mihailovitch. This idea came to him as he read of General Drazha Mihailovitch of the Yugoslav guerrilla forces.

For some years now people have been taking legal steps to recover their "right" names. One day in 1917 at Fort Snelling, Minnesota, a top sergeant calling the company roster paused and sputtered, "Gosh, George, I can't pronounce your name. I'll just call you Sprague." By some means which I, a one-time company clerk, don't understand, the top kick changed all the man's records to read "Sprague." The soldier was naturalized automatically under his new name. Twenty-odd years later, however, George Sprague appeared in a Chicago court. "I'm tired of being called by a name I was not born to," he said. "I want my real name again." He left the courtroom as George Stanislauskas.

On July 8, 1941, the United Press sent this item from Chicago: "Because his customers could never remember his name Louis Harris, a butcher, petitioned the court to change it back to Elias Haralampopoulas. Harris is a Greek, his customers are Greeks, and Harris, in Greek, is a difficult name."

On December 8, 1939, the *Chicago Tribune* published

on the front page a brief dispatch from its Milwaukee reporter: "Michael George Dansand, 39 years old, who changed his name from Domagalski in 1925, filed a petition in Circuit Court . . . to have his old name back."

A New England judge who has had several such cases during 1938-40 told me that most of the people who wanted their old names back insisted on the strictly correct old-country spelling—"as if in atonement," said the judge. One man who had apparently been "passing" as an old-time Yankee changed from Kent back to Dziatkiewicz.

The hostility on the part of "Americans" to "foreign" names is a factor in the continuance of the hundreds of Polonias, Hungaricas, Little Italys, Wop Roosts, Little Bohemias, Finntowns and other "foreign" sections in most of the larger cities in the United States.

Like Kobotchnik, many of the foreign-born—especially those who have come here in their twenties or later—are attached to their old-country cognomens and customs. So they stay in the "foreign" sections which in some respects are isolated from forces inimical to "foreign" names and, as such, serve as an escape from the necessity of coping with the problem. This is true also of some second-generation folk who are indisposed to change their handles.

PROMISCUOUS CHANGING FOR THE SAKE
OF A JOB

SOMETIMES members of the same family are known by two
or three or four different names, and the same persons have
several simultaneously or in sequence.

One immigrant whose old-country name is Gavrilo
Chernichenkoff owns a house as George Chernich, has an
insurance policy issued to Avrely Czernizen and is known
in the factory where he works as Mike Chern. One of his
sons is employed under the name of Chernoff, another
"passes" as Blackstone (*cherni* meaning "black") and two
more plus a daughter are plain Black. The last four
changed in order to get rid of the disadvantage of a "foreign" name in job-seeking.

This kind of haphazard shifting is accompanied by much
irritation and frequently is at once the cause and the result of deplorable intra-family relations. Sooner or later it
produces legal difficulties, whereupon the family sometimes gets together and formally establishes its name as
Black, say, or Chern or Chernoff. Such meetings, usually
in a lawyer's office, are frequently awkward and sometimes
painful, especially for the old man who brought the "foreign" name to America and is looked upon by his children
as a kind of villain. Sometimes he loses his temper and
refuses to go through with the formality. Or one of the
American-born sons suddenly holds out and remains
Chernoff, or even goes all the way back to Chernichenkoff,
"just for the hell of it," to annoy the others.

But often the family makes no effort to agree on the
question. It just disintegrates—a casualty of the battle of
names. The sons and daughters drift away and become

part of the great expanding pool of America's human mediocrity.

Promiscuous name-changing of this sort too often has a hand in producing negative personal developments. I know of young second-generation Americans of Slavic, Italian, Jewish, Lithuanian, and Hungarian derivation who, out of shame over being "foreigners" and for purposes of job-hunting, go under several different handles.

In six or seven years as an occasional industrial worker, the son of a Slavic immigrant family in Chicago had ten or a dozen names—he does not know the exact number himself. Looking for work in factories where employment managers "had it in for foreigners," or didn't want to bother with "foreign" cognomens, he gave one of his Anglo-Saxon or Irish or "American" aliases. Where foremen were Polish or Czech or German immigrants, he gave a Polish or Czech or German name. This system worked, for some immigrant or second-generation bosses favor people of their own background, just as old-stock American or English-immigrant job-givers prefer persons with Anglo-Saxon names. These divergent favoritisms strengthen one another.

By-and-by the young fellow was not always sure what his name was, or who he was, and "didn't care a hell of a lot." Sometimes he forgot under which tag he was supposed to be known at that particular time. He drifted into petty crime. In 1939 he was arrested twice and identified himself differently each time. He served two short jail sentences because the police did not connect the offenses. Thus he discovered that using different names was "a pretty good idea." It helped him to get away with things. If the judge who tried him the second time had known of his first confinement, he would have given him a stiffer sentence.

He left Chicago for Detroit, where he worked awhile

for a man who hated Catholics and "thought a lot" of him because he had given—around the time of the Russo-Finnish war—a Finnish name, implying that he was a Lutheran, although he was actually from a Catholic family. Toward the end of 1940 he was arrested in a stolen car in Toledo. His Chicago record caught up with him through fingerprints, and now he is doing a ten-year stretch. His story came to me through an official of the penitentiary.

I do not mean that using aliases in job-seeking is never justifiable, or that the practice always indicates a lack of character or a personal smash-up. It doesn't many times. A newspaperman friend tells me: "Almost every day an obituary comes in with something like this: 'Mr. Smith is survived by his father Mr. Stanislaw Smyzanski and his older brother Frank Smyzanski.' Nearly always the Anglicized name has been taken on by the man important enough to rate an obit, not by relatives mentioned in the notice."

Nor do I mean, of course, to cast any reflection on professional groups whose tradition it is to assume new names. Actors and writers, for instance. Perhaps half the stars in Hollywood have other names than they were born to.

I learn from the July, 1941, *Readers Digest* that the original name of Gypsy Rose Lee, the strip-tease star, was Rose Louise Hovick. She came by "Gypsy" through her early predilection for having her fortune told by gypsies. I suppose "Lee" is a re-formation of "Louise." And she dropped "Hovick" because it sounded too much like "havoc." (On the other hand, her sister, also an actress, calls herself June Havoc.) And when Gypsy got into movies and the Will Hays office received four thousand protests on the ground that a burlesque queen was unfit to appear in films, she changed back temporarily to Louise Hovick: it didn't matter—the customers were bound to recognize her body.

Well-known is the stage and screen actor Boris Karloff, who usually plays criminals, maniacs, monsters and ogres of all descriptions. He is London-born. His original name was Charles Edward Pratt, under which he started his acting career. For a time he was a matinee idol. "I know it's hard to believe," he said in an interview, "but before coming to New York I toured England in stock and I was the handsome hero who always got the girl. This is by no means to be taken as a reflection on the tastes or critical faculties of the English audiences—or of English girls. . . . In the United States I played in many road companies and then had small parts in the movies. But always I was a 'good guy.' . . . Then one day the actor who was originally scheduled to play *Frankenstein* couldn't, for some reason or other, and in desperation the producer let me try it. *I changed my name to make myself as much of a menace as possible. . . .*" The italics are mine. By taking the name of Boris Karloff in order to become a convincing "horror man," Mr. Pratt catered to the idea that foreigners are evil, and my guess is that thereby he unintentionally added to the difficulties of the "foreign"-named in the United States. But he was very much within the tradition of his profession, while proving, as he puts it, "that villainy can be as lucrative as virtue—on the screen" and inducing his audiences to think that "I was that sort of person in private life—a rare compliment" to an actor.

Industrial and white-collar workers, however, have no pseudonymal tradition, and with many—not all—the connection is close between easily assumed aliases and personal weakness or disintegration. Sometimes lack of character leads to aliases, sometimes alias-using becomes a germ of degeneration.

In a problem of this sort there is of course no way of arriving at truth in statistical form.

It is my impression, however, that the use of aliases in

employment-hunting has been diminishing (1937-42) along with radical name-changing generally. At the same time that they were getting rid of their sense of shame about being "Polacks" and "Hunkies" and "Greeks" and "Wops," many young people of immigrant parentage came to realize —during the depression—that getting a job was not easy for most young folk quite aside from any question of names. Being of foreign descent and known as Mikolajczak or Tsatsaronis or Somogyi or Kalpakjian or Paganelli was just one more factor in the general reality. They expected stiff competition. Many had faced the disadvantage of "foreign" names in school by excelling as students, by scrubbing their necks, by dressing as neatly as possible and behaving well. As job-seekers, they continued to follow the same tactic. Numbers of the second generation grew determined to get on in spite of their "foreign" handles. The drawback acted as a prod stimulating them to surpass others not so handicapped. This holds of course only for those who were challenged rather than depressed or crushed by an additional obstacle. The point at which a particular handicap ceases to stimulate and becomes a weight varies with the individual, and a "foreign" name in surroundings inimical to it is no exception.

Beginning with the first half of 1941, as mass production for "Defense" got under way and the war feeling grew, the difficulties of some of the "foreign"-named working people increased. Employment managers in armament factories eyed them suspiciously and questioned them closely; especially those managers who were themselves of the new strains and had an inner need to emphasize their Americanism at no matter whose expense.

A mill superintendent in western Pennsylvania, a second-generation Austrian-German American with an Anglicized name, needed constant documentation—in his own eyes— that he was a one-hundred-percent-plus American. Perhaps his experience as a son of a German immigrant during the First World War had been unpleasant. At any rate, for a while he would not hire anyone whose grandfather had not been born in the United States. Finally his board of directors, mostly old-stock Americans, overruled him.

Here and there, through most of 1941, industries filling British and United States "Defense" and "Lend-Lease" orders discriminated against owners of "foreign" names who sought jobs. This was not necessarily because the superintendents and employment managers were themselves prejudiced. Often they knew that Jack Brunowitz was a hundred-per cent loyal and a good worker. Yet they did not hire him because the men working in their plants interested British agents, the Federal Bureau of Investigation and the Army and Navy Intelligence who—unfortunately none too well informed about the immigrant groups—were apt to ask many questions about employees with such names, which took a lot of precious time to answer. It was simpler, easier, not to engage them, especially since there was still a large supply of unemployed labor from which to draw.

In 1940-41 such circumstances, rising out of emergency-created suspicions, drove some immigrants and second-generation people to tentative aliases and legal name-changing. But many adhered to their policy, discussed in the preceding chapter, of not yielding to hysteria and prejudice.

After Pearl Harbor this policy was strengthened by the increase in red tape and formality in connection with employment in war industries. Would-be war-industry workers had to show birth certificates, which gave their original names; fill out long questionnaire-applications, which they had to swear to; and give references of people who usually knew them by the names of Anagnostopoulos, Frzysztacki, Mantzoros, Kovachnik, Jontez, Ljubomorovitz, Mlodzian-owski, Kulbokas, Kruglak, Pihodna, Snoj, Subasich ——

TEACHERS CALLED THEM JOHNNY SNEEZE-IT AND FRANKIE WHOSIS

GLANCING back at the 1930's, I recall the story of a young woman of Czech parentage in the Middle West. Her name was originally very consonantal: Svrček. In public school, with her parents' reluctant consent, she modified it to Svorchek, which helped a little; people found it easier to pronounce. She tried not to be hurt when people occasionally still stumbled over it, but sometimes when the stumbler happened to be a teacher she couldn't help feeling miserable or annoyed. Then she would grit her teeth and study hard.

In college her real troubles began. One instructor took a perverse delight in deliberately sputtering over her name; another had the habit of raising his eyebrows only when addressing her. She suffered agonies, especially after she saw a student mimic the eyebrow-lifting professor. She thought of quitting the course, of giving up college altogether. But she stuck it out, and before the end of her sophomore year came to be regarded as one of the most brilliant students in the place.

She was particularly good in English. "From her appearance and speech," one of her classmates wrote me, "no one would have guessed that her parents spoke broken English when they spoke it at all. . . . In her senior year, when she applied for a teaching position and was urged to change her name, she remained Svorchek. She graduated with highest honors in her class and two years later got a good position. Now in her mid-twenties, highly respected by her colleagues and pupils, she teaches English and dramatics in the high school in the small Illinois city where her family lives."

Miss Svorchek's teachers are not entitled to much credit. Generally, however, teachers have greatly improved. More intelligent about "foreigners," many now exercise an important influence in reducing the drastic shame that leads to name-changing among the second generation.

In the 1920's it was—according to numerous accounts— almost common practice on the part of teachers particularly, it seems, in Pittsburgh and vicinity, Chicago, Cleveland and Detroit to humiliate pupils with "difficult" names. Many made next to no effort to pronounce them correctly. Some did not trouble to pronounce them at all. I know men who were called, for example, Johnny Sneeze-it and Frankie Whosis in school instead of Johnny Rodzinski and Frankie Wojciekowski. One man tells me he went through a year in high school known as The Boy with the Long Name, then quit largely because of that; and his name, Vankovsky, is not difficult.

Twenty or fifteen years ago, and more recently, all too many schools had all too many teachers who thought the "foreign kids" ought to be glad they had a school to come to; why should the teachers go to any extra trouble for them? There was plenty to do with the "American" youngsters, who were entitled to consideration; their parents' taxes paid their salaries, erroneously implying that immigrants were not taxpayers. These "foreign" brats were backward, poor-looking, insecure, furtive, and weak in English—an all-around nuisance.

This concept was tied to the anti-alien sentiment rampant in the United States for nearly a decade after the First World War. To many principals and teachers the great number of "foreign" youngsters in the schools was an extra burden, a documentation of the notion that the country was going to the dogs. Their names were the most irritating thing about the "foreign kids," perhaps because the most obvious marks of their "foreignness."

In many schools, of course, this was not true; at least not so baldly. But in some to my personal knowledge it still holds.

By and large, however, particularly since about 1935, there has been a great change over nearly all of the country. A growing number of teachers—among them most of those who, like Miss Svorchek, are themselves of immigrant parentage—have begun to see in the augmenting numbers of second-generation boys and girls a challenge and an opportunity. As a start, they are helping one another to realize that—as Mrs. Pearl Cessna Kellogg, a teacher in Fresno County, California, writes me—"when an Armenian family changes from Bedrosian to Peterson, or from Hagopian to Jacobs, it implies a lack of pride in ancestral background, and it widens the rift between older and younger generations, already so difficult to bridge in immigrant families." They take care that children are not embarrassed on account of their names. They are learning to pronounce and spell them, and they do their best to inspire respect for them in other pupils.

This development came in conjunction with all the others in the problem of names during the last decade: the favorable newspaper publicity some of the "old countries" received in the United States; such books as *Madame Curie, Musa Dagh,* and *Old Jules* which many teachers have read; and the resultant increased self-assurance of many immigrant parents which gave them the courage to complain to school principals and urge a better attitude toward their children.

There were other influences in this process which I have not yet mentioned. One was the rise to prominence, in the late twenties and through the thirties, of good and able men of foreign birth or descent—the late Mayor Anton Cermak, United States Circuit Court of Appeals Judge

Otto Kerner, and Federal Reserve Governor M. S. Szymczak of Chicago; Mayor Frank Lausche of Cleveland; and
Mayor La Guardia and Judge Pecora of New York, to mention only a few. As political leaders or high civic officials
they began to influence the schools. In New York City
the former president of the Board of Education, James
Marshall, himself a second-generation American, delivered
before teacher groups some pertinent addresses on the problems of immigrants and their native-American children.

To whatever causes it may be ascribed, this development
in schools and individual teachers now continues on its own
sound legs and is probably the most important source of
energy in dealing sensibly with "foreign" names.

Not that even the most well-intentioned, competent principals and teachers always find it easy to be intelligent
and patient. Sometimes the problem is bewildering enough
to strain anyone's nerves. Often the spelling and pronunciation differ in the same family. Sometimes children spell
and pronounce their names differently at different times,
depending on their moods and whims, on the state of
their inferiority feelings at the moment or on the argument
with their parents at the dinner table the evening before.
Or cousins with names spelled exactly the same insist on
different pronunciations: one perhaps the old-country
form, the others blundering efforts to bring it within the
frame of English speech. This sort of thing occasionally
forces the teacher to take a hand or the principal to call
a convention of the parents concerned. If no agreement is
reached, he may have to establish one pronunciation for
the whole clan. This happened to my knowledge with a
group of French-Canadian families in a school in Massachusetts some years ago.

It is not what I call organic procedure but, out of sym-
pathy for teachers who are trying to be considerate and
intelligent, one cannot be intolerant of it. In most cases it
is ultimately accepted with grace and gratitude. Where dif-

ficulties continue, they are often due to archaic hangovers in the parents of which teachers and principals are unaware but to which the children continue to react.

My friend William Suchy, a young teacher at the Sterling Morton Junior High School in Cicero, Illinois, writes: "My experience with 'foreign' names is rather humorous." He is of Czech-immigrant parentage and is familiar with Slavic pronunciation. "When I started teaching, I just naturally tended to pronounce Czech and Polish names somewhat accurately. The resentment of the pupils forced me to learn the accepted mispronunciations which have been established by old-stock teachers."

Where an unsympathetic attitude regarding "foreign" names persists in the classroom, the fault is not always the teacher's. In too many places members of boards of education and their executives are petty politicians. Some are alien-baiters or revert to primitivism in other ways. Some, like the employment manager of the preceding chapter, are "passing" as old-stock Americans and exaggerating their Americanism. But their influence in local affairs is so powerful that teachers lacking in independence or character follow their example. Among such teachers are second-generation individuals with Anglicized names who in a sort of blind drive to justify themselves would like to see all other "foreigners" Anglicize theirs.

I do know of schools, however, where individual teachers manage to give play to their intelligence and judgment even in unfavorable circumstances. Here are two examples:

"For a couple of years I had charge of the school paper in the Farragut High School in Chicago," writes Mr. M. E. Stevenson, now director of a summer camp in Upper Michigan. "The pupils were mostly children of Bohemian immigrants; their names lent themselves to many twists, and the non-Bohemian youngsters loved to take cracks at them. The witticisms were mostly like the sports writers' gags kidding football players named Szaczytkowize and Antzpanski, but I noticed that some touched the victims, especially the girls, to the quick.

"In adolescence it is difficult to appreciate such humor; so I called a conference of the newspaper kids . . . and we decided that thenceforth there would be no ribbing about names. The argument ran like this: if you were young, you could not do very much about your name; it was inherited, like the color of your hair or the shape of your nose. . . .

"This line went over big and spread through the school, and there was no more trouble. Occasionally teachers would talk to kids with extremely difficult names, and to their parents; then the family might decide to simplify them, usually over a summer vacation so the change would not draw too much attention. The simplifications, however, did not go unnoticed by others whose names were tough. They took the hint, spoke to their folks, and eventually they modified their names too, in most cases retaining some semblance of the Bohemian original."

In a New England town that is three-fourths "foreign," one teacher follows this method: "Right after I assign seats I go up and down the aisles with my seating plan, copying names from the pupils' programs. I ask each one to pronounce his name for me, no matter how easy it may be. I repeat it, deliberately mispronouncing one or two simple ones. I show each student his name after writing it in and ask if it is down correctly. I make mistakes, intentional and otherwise, with difficult and simple names alike. I write the pronunciations phonetically. And when this is all on paper, I tell my repertory of stories, picked up mostly in the Boston and New York public libraries, the point of which is that some of the most common American names are hard to pronounce for the French in France or the Czechs in Bohemia. There is a difference of opinion as to some of them—Gannett, for one—even in this country. I try to guess how Wilson, say, or Granger or Lewis or Burroughs would fare on the tongues of Bulgarians, Magyars, or Italians in their home countries. This proves very interesting to my sixth-grade youngsters.

"Then I go through the names on my seating plan, continuing to make mistakes and being corrected. On second reading I try to get all the names right. Of course I still falter over Mnatsekanian, Jendriczk and Gianninoto, and again I ask for help. There are grins in the class; I smile myself, but try to appear embarrassed, not amused. Sometimes a sensitive pupil shrugs his shoulders in apparent indifference when I inquire if my pronunciation is correct; or he exclaims grimly, 'Nobody gets it right, like my father says it's right, so what's the use!'

"By now the class is fascinated. Some of the students become very much interested in the pronunciation problem, which has turned into a kind of sport: and when one of them puts over 'Gianninoto,' he is apt to remark triumphantly, 'Gee, I got it that time, didn't I?' or 'Pretty cute, ain't it!' After this there is not likely to be any unpleasantness in or out of the classroom on account of names.

"I practice the hard ones at home. Occasionally I get one I can't manipulate at all. I had a rip-snorter last year. I confessed my inability to the boy and asked if I could call him by his first name, Sylvester. He was an agreeable chap who, so far as I could detect, had no inner quirk about it; he grinned and said, 'Sure'; then he signed his papers 'Sylvester.' We became good friends, and after a while he told me that his family wouldn't shorten the name before his grandfather died—he was an old man and thought 'an awful lot of the darned name.'

"Now and then I get a name which may be all right in the old country but which sounds embarrassing here and goes terribly against my New England grain, and which ought to be changed—to anything, just so it is changed!"

SOME OUGHT TO BE CHANGED, BUT—

THERE can be no argument that names which have unesthetic or offensive connotations in English ought to be replaced—preferably by something that will not obscure their linguistic background. I know a House who was once Backhaus, and an ex-Lipschitz whose father, in the days when the *Shamrocks* were winning all the yacht races, changed to Lipton. On entering college a young Jewish American whose father's name also was Lipschitz took his mother's maiden name, Sundell, whereupon the rest of the family followed suit. Incidentally, it seems to me that taking the mother's name if it is intrinsically preferable, even in cases where the father's name is not unesthetic but only difficult, is an excellent idea, provided the change does not gripe the father too much.

Dr. Edward G. Punkay of Chicago writes me that his name was originally spelled Punke in German. In English the silent *e* gave it an undesirable sound and meaning, "which would have been a ball-and-chain around my neck," so he altered it to Punkay—fairly close to the original German pronunciation and in line with the organic procedure I favor.

In 1941 in Omaha, Nebraska, the joke-weary Bovio Palucca asked court permission to adopt Parke.

In the late 1930's and early 40's the names of some of the Axis leaders and their quislings were poison. In New York City a Duce became Duke; in Hartford, Connecticut, a Ribbentropp took the name of Robinson; in Rochester, New York, a court allowed Tony Musolino to become Tony Mason; and in Chicago a house-painter changed from Hitler to Gitler. In mid-June, 1942, *Variety* reported that, "to avoid any possible confusion with Hitler's collaborator Pierre Laval," the well-known NBC orchestra leader Paul Laval decided to spell his name Lavalle.

I have mentioned the soldiers named Hitler who declined revision. The retort of one, "Let the other guy change it!" gave me a laugh; it is quite all right so far as I am concerned if he wishes to remain Hitler. The connotation of this name is such, however (and I trust it will never improve), that I would not try to dissuade anyone from discarding it for almost anything else.

Such changing is demanded by irresistible forces which appear from time to time or have permanent existence in the country's general atmosphere. In most cases, this method of alteration—while perhaps not one-hundred-percent organic at first glance—is less damaging to personality than retention of the objectionable name. In fact, if the person involved is blessed with sufficient common sense and perspective on the subject, the change may become quite organic through a clear realization of its necessity.

But I limit my unequivocal approval of such changing only to names with esthetically and politically objectionable connotations.

During the First World War great numbers of Germans and German Americans hastily Anglicized their names although most of them were easy to manage. The reasons were obvious and not restricted to the United States. They operated in England, where—as an example—Prince Louis Alexander of Battenberg, a German who became a naturalized Briton and served 51 years in the British Navy, found it necessary in 1917 to translate his name to Mountbatten, passing the translation onto his son, the present Lord Louis Mountbatten.

In the 1920's and 1930's many German Americans changed back again. But in the early 1940's discrimination began to affect German Americans (as well as Italian Americans) once more, including here and there second- and even third-generation people whose names were still un-touched, and translation and transliteration into English are noticeable again. In May, 1941, a man named Kaiser petitioned a court in Los Angeles to change to King "for the sake of my five children."

This seems to me inorganic, no matter how one looks at it. There is hysteria; there is giving in to fear, although much less than in 1917-18. And I suspect that such chang-ing often occurs through yielding too readily to sharp but quite local prejudice. The victim named Kaiser, say, does not realize that outside of his neighborhood many Kaisers in various parts of the country have no trouble on account of their name. Three are in the 1942-43 *Who's Who in America*: one a famous physician in Rochester, New York; one the public librarian and one a construction engineer and industrialist in Oakland, California. The last has been connected with the Boulder, Bonneville and Grand Coulee dams, was the subject of a series of articles in *The Satur-day Evening Post* in the late spring of 1941, and is cur-rently engaged in executing huge war contracts given him by the Government mainly because he has proved his abil-ity to get things done.

But inorganic alteration of this sort—not only of Ger-man but of any "foreign" names—has the hearty approval of many Anglo-Saxon old-stock Americans and of the "Americanized" one-hundred-percent-plus-ers as well.

One of my correspondents, a Los Angeles physician, sug-gests a federal law requiring all persons with "foreign" names now here to Anglicize them at once. He would have all new immigrants similarly afflicted "park their handles" in a large card index at Ellis Island, where they would be assigned new appellations like Jones, Dewey, Adams, Buck-ley, Phillips, Sims, Woods, Weston and Lockley. I am aware of others who have equally thoroughgoing ideas even if their programs are less concrete. A lady has written me expressing full approval of a Jewish merchant family in Virginia for changing from Witz to Whitney. She maintains with logic very satisfactory to herself that by following this example Jews would take an intelligent step against anti-Semitism. And hundreds of letters which have come to me from all over the country run somewhat like this one, which came from Hollywood:

"A fellow in our office named Siegelbauer recently swapped his name for Sinclair. We all discussed the matter, and we ended up in strong agreement that all foreigners with tongue-twisting names who aim to stay here (as distinct from people with simple handles) should change them at once. Names like Przybsewski are an affront to national harmony, and an outrage to second-generation Americans. Siegelbauer is not very hard and he could have got along okay with it; but we all thought the change was wise.

"Furthermore, we came to the conclusion that we did not blame old-line American school youngsters for teasing kids whose stupid parents, from misguided Old World patriotism or for whatever reason, make them hang onto names like Gzbelsuebzgy. It's a natural instinct; and instead of lambasting the American children for teasing the foreigners the immigrant parents ought to catch it for not doing something about their name. They are settled in America, whose basic culture is essentially Anglo-Saxon, and whose language is English. The stubborn, prideful hanging onto the old-country monickers prevents many acceptable immigrants and immigrants' children from getting along better.

"This name business is a real problem. I admit I no longer feel the old oddness in the presence of jaw-breaking names; now I feel annoyed, impatient, irritated because they have not been fixed. A change implies so far as I am concerned no knuckling under, no giving up of one's background, but a refusal to change signifies indifference or arrogance, or childish pride in national origin. It's like advertising one's culture: 'Look, I'm a Pole! Ain't I wonderful?' or, 'Look, my people came from Armenia!'—which is cheap and silly.

"My impression is that the old prejudice against a name because it is foreign has largely passed; the prejudice now is not against the foreign origin of the person, but against the sound of a name which is uneuphonious, unharmonious in the American scene. An American like myself whose name may be Smith or Hill or Lucas is conscious of this disharmony. And it rubs him the wrong way. His friend may be as smooth and gracious and 'belonging' as anybody, but if he has a tough name, there arises a distinct discordance in their relationship. In introducing him there will always be on the part of the old-stock American, however well he may conceal it, a certain self-consciousness. There are wicked little psychological barriers. . . . I insist: it is the brash lack of euphony, the tinpanny disharmony, that is mainly at the bottom of the American 'prejudice' against impossible, un-vowelled foreign names.

"People named Czyzewski or Mrgudich or Hlovocek or Tomaszewski fail to realize that they are no longer in Poland or the Ukraine, in Lithuania or the Balkans, but in a country whose language is simple and liquid with many vowels. Freedom to call oneself by an unpronounceable name is not freedom at all. In effect it is a restriction on the newcomer and on those who have long preceded him here.

"Many foreign names of course do not any longer seem foreign, for they are quite reasonable. Cermak is okay. Dominguez is okay. I am even getting used to Biscailuz, the name of the Sheriff of Los Angeles County who is of Swiss or Basque stock. Garbo is okay too, of course. . . . In fact, some foreign names are downright charming, easy to pronounce and remember, and they strike no discordant note in English speech. But I wish you would do what you can to induce the owners of the difficult, uneuphonious ones to change them. . . ."

With several of the points in this letter I partly agree; with some, almost entirely. I agree that "foreign" names rub many old-stock people the wrong way. But how much of this is due to the names themselves and how much to the old-American idea, still widespread, that the country is strictly Anglo-Saxon and to its corollary that the non-Anglo-Saxon elements should quickly seek to conform? My correspondent accepts Cermak, Dominguez, Garbo and "even" Biscailuz as "reasonable." But he does not know apparently that to large sections of old-stock America, as well as to many in non-Slavic groups, "Cermak" too is objectionable. Will he let the several Cermaks in Chicago keep their name? What will he do about those who continue to object to it? How will he end the disharmony? Where does "reasonableness" as to names begin and end? *Whose* "reason" is going to approve which name? And when? Now? Or can we wait awhile? If we wait awhile, isn't it possible that some of the names which may now seem "difficult" will be quite "reasonable" in time? If so, why not just be a little patient?

These questions may seem like quibbling. The trouble is, we do not meet on "reasonable" ground when we consider the name problem. I have indicated that one of the strongest impulses in it has nothing to do with reason. It is intensely personal, subjective; it is—in part, at least—primitive. It may be foolish but it is strong. It's a battle.

In common with nearly all others who have written to me on the subject, my correspondent too is personal, subjective. He suggests that "foreign" names bother him less than they used to. Why? Apparently several of the simpler ones have become familiar to him; *ergo,* "reasonable" and "downright charming." Now even Biscailuz is not too much for him. I think that if a Mrgudich should suddenly write a best seller, win the heavyweight championship of the world, save the President from a would-be assassin as did Tony Cermak, or sink a Japanese battleship, his name might become familiar to him too; whereupon he might accept it and pronounce it in his stride, as I do—it is a Yugoslav name and so no trouble to me at all.

But by this I do not mean that Mrgudich should not simplify his name and make things a little easier for the country. I think he should—no less than should Carl Elmer Ahrenhoersterbaeumer of St. Louis.

PRINCE MDIVANI, HEINZ' PICKLES, AND ZPHGASYLZOWITCH

THE problem of names is intertwined with economic and social circumstances.

Before me is a membership list of the Colonial Dames of America, descendants of public officials in the Colonies before the Revolution. In it I find such names as de Raasloff, de Ropp, Ehrenclon, Krainik, Majewski, Milewsky-Milevitch, Zaugg, Pincoffs, Mkhalapov, Heitzelmann, von Maohrenschildt, Esberg, Harshbarger, and Zug. A safe guess is that riches or titles accompanied most of the "foreign" names these Dames married, for in the eyes of many upper-class Americans the possessor of a title and wealth is automatically less foreign than an untitled, unopulent person with an even less difficult name than Mkhalapov or Milewsky-Milevitch. If one's name is Mdivani and one is alleged to be a Georgian prince with some money of his own, Americans on Park Avenue or at Palm Beach find him "simply fascinating." Such names, or I should say names of such people, seem to have no trouble getting into the Social Register in which I find Baltazzi, Dimitriu, Jarecki, Smirnoff, de Tarnowsky, von Peccoz, Zazulinski, Travelletti, Krausnick, Niedringhaus, Piroumoff, Afflerback, Wolkowski, Peixotto, Eilshiminus, de Chelminski, Jaccaci, Iznard, Maximov, Obolensky, Melhado, Sausoni, Taliaferro, Theodoli, Tjaarda, Tjader, Voislawski, de Bakhtiar, de Kozlowski, de Bourcia, de Shauensee, Tomacelli, Torchiana, Wielopolski, Kovakenko, Flaccus, and Nimick. And there is probably very little stumbling over the name of David Sarnoff, not only because it is comparatively easy but because its owner is a great tycoon. Success, money and power can work wonders. Someone has said that the most alien person in America is the poor man. If in addition his name is Pincoffs or Majewski or Krainik, he is apt to be a two-legged threat to everything American although he may be a native of Wilkes-Barre, Pennsylvania, or Stillwater, Oklahoma, or he may speak English with less of an accent than some of the husbands of the Colonial Dames, whose married names are probably the secret envy of not a few of their sisters in and out of the organization who are plain Mrs. Smiths and Mrs. Joneses.

I agree with John Switalski, whose views are paraphrased in an earlier chapter, that many of the stupidities now part of the name problem will vanish as the general conditions of American life draw closer to equalization.

In 1927 Francesca Vinciguerra, a native of Sicily who had been brought to the United States when not quite three, had her first novel, *The Ardent Flame*, accepted by the late Century Company. But the publishers were so disturbed by the thought of such "a long and difficult" name on the backstrip of a highly poetical romantic novel, and had so many misgivings about sales when the customers tried to pronounce it, that they suggested changing it. The young novelist appreciated their realistic view of the matter and, rather reluctantly, cast about for a pen name—reluctantly because her family had called itself Vinciguerra since the eleventh century, and the name of one of her ancestors appears in biographies of St. Francis. "Finally," the writer now well-known as Frances Winwar told me fifteen years later, "I hit on a compromise. I kept my name—in translation. *Vinci* means 'win,' *guerra* is 'war': hence Winwar."

Generally, though, "foreign" names are no handicap in the arts. By and large, they are an advantage—witness the one-time Oklahoma cowboy who as Benton got nowhere in the singing world but became a success as Bentonelli.

This is true of many musicians. Also of painters and writers. Mencken has pointed out that the roster of the National Institute of Arts and Letters includes Beaux, Becker, Benet, Cortissoz, Damrosch, Dielman, Du Mond, Ferber, Groll, Guerin, Hagedorn, Johansen, Jennewein, Keller, Kroeger, Kroll, Laessle, La Farge, Lefevre, Lie, Loeffler, Marr, Niehaus, Oldberg, Patigian, Repplier, Roth, Sandburg, Schelling, Speicher, Sterner, Stock, Stoessel, Volk, Vonnoh, Weinman and Wister.

Socially, if they mingle mainly with people in their own professional sphere, "foreign"-named artists and writers encounter no difficulty, as suggested by the story of Stoyan Pribichevich. There was no unkind reaction to his name in the literary circles of New York but an almost general eagerness to learn it. Most people he met at literary parties were either fairly well-to-do or above the average in a certain kind of cosmopolitan intelligence.

To some extent this applies—in spite of Miss Svorchek's professors—to faculty people in most American colleges and universities. Which is important, for the number of "foreign" names on student rosters has been rapidly increasing for years. Professor P. Marston of the University of New Hampshire writes that non-English names "do attract my attention . . . but many of these students I count among my best friends. After knowing them awhile their names cease to be strange."

A University of Illinois professor, however, writes: "I must admit a prejudice for English names. Such names as Szubra or Czerny strike me as strange and fall hesitatingly from my tongue—if I can negotiate them at all. They place me at a disadvantage which I consider unnecessary. I have no quarrel with Adamic or Stadthagen; they indicate their origin but I can pronounce them easily. I may not give them the approved accent, but I can do well enough."

On the upper levels of the world of science and learning the spelling and sound of names is of no consequence.

There is hardly a college or university of any standing that hasn't at least a few professors with "foreign" names. In fact, many institutions of higher learning are extremely friendly to foreign-born and second-generation instructors and quite unconcerned about their names. But most of them would rather have a Professor Gorkowski in the Science than in the English or American History Department.

In the secondary schools there is a great deal of resistance to aspiring teachers with "foreign" patronymics. The majority of teachers' colleges and normal schools are urging young would-be pedagogues who are sons and daughters of Slavic, Greek, Italian, Lithuanian, or Armenian immigrants to Anglicize or to modify their family names before graduation. School boards and superintendents in most cities and counties tend to be anti-"foreign" and do not want teachers named Jerabek, Zerzedies, Pawlyshyn, Zsipay, and Zamblaoskas. Many young teachers do Anglicize their names to get jobs; others don't either because they resent the manner in which this "advice" is given or because they can't for vital personal reasons. Many fail to find positions, but some, by virtue of ability and character and luck, do get them anyhow.

In recent years, however, this pressure too has seemed to decrease—thanks in part to the administration of Mayor C. D. Scully, even in Pittsburgh, which until the late 1930's was one of the worst cities in this respect. And it may be that—along with other developments in the entire situation—as more and more "foreign"-named teachers prove their abilities, their successors will be required less and less to discard non-English surnames in order to become American teachers.

This goes, too, for private schools—in spite of the "Pedrotti" case described in the letter I quote at the outset of this book.

That the same trend exists in Canada came clearly to

light in the summer of 1941 after the school board of Hampton, a town near Bowmanville, Ontario, had engaged Mae Kozak, a native Canadian of Canadian-Ukrainian origin. A majority of the ratepayers protested the appointment on the basis that Miss Kozak "is a child of foreign-born parents while our armies are at war with the Baltic States." Some of the signatories complained too that the young lady was "an Italian and a Catholic." Actually, as the *Toronto Daily Star* (August 12) had it in a leading editorial, she was "a 19-year-old Canadian girl of exceptional ability, a member of the Uniate Church, and the sister of a Canadian with Canada's forces overseas." Under pressure, the school board of Hampton annulled the appointment; but this is not the important thing in the case. Important is that she immediately got a teaching job in another town, and that the press all over Ontario took the people of Hampton to task for their action. *The Peterborough Examiner* said that the incident "falls readily into a class of things which we might sincerely wish had never taken place in Ontario or anywhere else in Canada. It does not get down and walk on all fours with our ideas of freedom and tolerance." *The St. Thomas Times-Journal* thought that "if the loyalty of Canadians is to be challenged because of a name which may have been passed on to them from a father, grandfather, or great-grandfather, a lot of fine citizens should, by the Hamptonian standard, have to beg their bread from door to door. Or be in internment camps. Even some of our members of parliament [named Hlynka, Bercovitch, Hoblitzell, etc.] could not survive a Hamptonian vendetta against 'furrin' names."

Manners, mannerisms and general behavior have a great deal to do with whether or not people at large accept "foreign" names.

In the more "refined" circles in the East there appears to be less tendency to regard foreign-born Judge Ferdinand

Pecora as an Italian than Fiorello La Guardia, who is a native Arizonan, partly because La Guardia's mannerisms are more dramatic, less restrained, and therefore less "American" and more "Italian" than Pecora's. Wendell Willkie is a second-generation German American, but his personality, speech and behavior are so thoroughly American in the contemporaneous sense that hardly any of the old-stock people think of him as anything else. He might, however, be less completely accepted if his name were, say, Schwartzenkopf.

In the political sphere there are regions where a "foreign" name is an advantage, provided you are willing to limit your career as to elective offices. In Minnesota candidates with Scandinavian names are favored; indeed, the saying goes that nobody with an Anglo-Saxon name could be elected governor of that state. Throughout the country there are city councilmen and mayors and state legislators with such names as Blatnik, Vrhovnik, Rossi, La Guardia; members and ex-members of the House of Representatives named Marcantonio, Boileau, Cavicchia, Dickstein, Dondero, Palmisano, Sadowski, Romjue, Tenerowicz, Kocialkowski, Maciejewski, Lesinski; and past and present Governors Lehman, Olson, Seligmann, Horner, and Petersen; but the most "foreign" names now in the United States Senate are Bilbo, La Follette, Van Nuys, Wagner, Vandenberg and Chavez.

In many places a "foreign" name bars one from running for the pettiest office. In 1939 John Ladesich, a Croatian American living in Pittsburgh, long active as a worker in the local Democratic party, thought he would like to try for an unimportant county job. He asked David Lawrence, Pennsylvania State Democratic chairman, to endorse him, and received the following reply: "John, I admit you are fully qualified for the office you aspire to. There is nothing wrong with your character, reputation or ability, but we are simply not endorsing any candidates with foreign names. I made that mistake four years ago and I am not going to make it twice."

Where prejudice is as strong as in Pittsburgh, many would-be politicos of new-immigrant derivation Anglicize their names. With few exceptions such men are mediocre, propelled by desire for self-advancement and subjected to the inner twists common to people who change their names inorganically, from dubious motives. It is in their character to yield to pressure from dominant groups. They assume the fronts expected of them. They "play the game."

The first-rate men with "foreign" names who attain to political leadership outside their group do not hide their origins or yield to prejudice. They go along as they are and work as hard and as well as possible at whatever they get a chance to do. Their ability is gradually recognized. The community gets used to their names and doesn't mind some confusion as to pronunciation. They just naturally become leaders. One of the best current examples is Frank J. Lausche of Cleveland. His parents were immigrants from Slovenia. His name, like "Roosevelt," is pronounced two or three different ways; neither he nor anyone else cares which is "correct." Always himself, he did an excellent job on the bench and in civic affairs; in 1941 he was elected Mayor; and, still in his early forties, he has become one of the most highly respected men in his native city.

In Washington many non-elective positions, high and low, are held by "foreign"-named people. Those in the lesser Civil Service jobs felt during 1940-41 a good deal of prejudice in their immediate superiors; but on the upper levels of government officialdom there was no sign of any discrimination against "foreigners." As I write, Leo Pasvolsky is a special assistant to the Secretary of State, and W. S. Woytivsky is a Social Security Board economist.

There are of course successful businessmen and financiers and industrialists with "foreign" names. I have mentioned

David Sarnoff. Also Henry J. Kaiser, of the West Coast, who in 1942 became all-important in the country's war shipbuilding program. There are William Knudsen and Sam Zemurray. The Weyerhaeuser lumber firm in the Northwest is well known. In Cleveland is my friend Frank Vlchek, the tool manufacturer. There are the German-named brewers. Certain luxury products—cheeses and wines, for instance—exploit the snob appeal of imported goods. Art and antique dealers are not handicapped, nor are beauty salons, haberdashery stores, restaurants, hotels and resorts.

Walter B. Weisenburger is the executive vice-president of the National Association of Manufacturers, in whose membership list occur many "foreign" names:

F. Hamachek, Jr., President, F. Hamachek Machine Co., Kewanee, Wis.

W. J. Serrotte, Treasurer, Bay West Paper Co., Green Bay, Wis.

Harry Dickstein, Anthracite Overall Manufacturing Co., Scranton.

S. J. Fehrenbach, Assistant Treasurer, Speer Carbon Co., St. Marys, Pa.

C. B. Leinendecker, Stroh Process Steel Co., Pittsburgh.

F. J. Hinderliter, Hinderliter Tool Co., Tulsa.

A. Arutunoff, Reda Pump Co., Bartlesville, Okla.

J. C. Argentsinger, Youngstown Sheet & Tube Co., Youngstown.

A. J. Jankowski, The Ohio Injector, Wadsworth, Ohio.

Jacob Sapirstein, American Greeting Publishers, Cleveland.

Henry L. Van Praag, Julius Kayser & Co., New York.

S. W. Fenollosa, General Offset Co., New York.

A. E. Bastedo, Burnham Boiler Corp., Irvington, N. Y.

J. W. Dittenheffer, Cortland Line Co., Inc., Cortland, N. Y.

L. P. Nemzek, Corpo Shoe Machinery Corp., Boston.

H. J. Lebherz, President, The Everedy Co., Frederick, Md.

R. G. Bellezza, Locke Insulator Corp., Baltimore.

H. W. Bockhoff, President, National Automatic Tool Co., Richmond, Ind.

C. U. Gramelspacher, Jasper Wood Products Co., Jasper, Ind.

Milton M. Latta, Western Rubber Co., Goshen, Ind.

M. P. Vachulka, Schick-Johnson Co., Chicago.

A. T. Huizinga, Montgomery Ward & Co., Chicago.

F. J. Matousek, Nemecek Bros., Chicago.

Clarence Wimpfheimer, The American Velvet Co., Stonington, Conn.

I could extend this list. On the whole, however, the American business world is intolerant of "foreign" names. This is especially true of big business, where names often become trade-marks, and trade-marks must be simple and rhythmic to the eye and ear, and easy on the tongue. Kellogg's Corn Flakes and Campbell Soups probably would not be so successful were they called Litwiniak Corn Flakes and Mesojednik Soups. Heinz is "foreign," but it is simple and short; if the pickle concern were named Mastrodomenico or Reinschreiber it might not have grown into the vast enterprise it is now.

In most big industrial firms and business offices, people called Zablodowski, Shumeyko, Koondakjian, Szymansarki, Krisztian, Grskovich, Degyanszky, Papavassilioy or Trinajstovich are virtually barred, regardless of their ability, from advancement to positions of authority and responsibility in which they would come in contact with the public. By and large, firms do not want their outgoing correspondence to bear such signatures. They do not want their customers to hesitate over names—and then place orders elsewhere. So most of the immigrants and second-generation people who aspire to executive business positions are required to change their names. Some houses do not take on "foreigners" for white-collar jobs under any circumstances. Or they bar Catholics or Jews or both. One company permitting no Catholics on its office force was outwitted by a Slavic-Catholic American youth of my acquaintance who appropriated a name common among Anglo-Saxon-Protestant New Englanders and has been "passing" ever since. In Budd Schulberg's interesting novel, *What Makes Sammy Run?*, Sammy Glick—altered from Shmelka Glickstein—got around one employer who refused to hire Jewish messenger boys. When his brother Israel, just ahead of him in the line of applicants, was turned away, Sammy knocked him down. "The dirty kike cut in ahead of me," he explained, then broke into gibberish Italian, cursing his resemblance to "them sheenies."

I have referred to the Einstein boys who became Easton with an eye to advancement in the Army and Navy; also—earlier in the book—to the general situation regarding names in our armed forces. I have said the Army has no definite policy on the problem, but the prejudice which exists in civilian life extends, naturally, to the military service.

The "foreign"-named soldier faces a handicap, but ability, good behavior and persistence can overcome it. One of our current lieutenant generals is Walter Krueger (who is, indeed, a native of Germany). The Adjutant General is James A. Ulio. There are at least two other generals—brigadiers when I last heard of them—with "foreign" names: Joseph E. Barzinski, son of Polish immigrants, in the Quartermaster Corps; and Haig Shekerjian, born in Armenia, one of the outstanding officers in the Chemical Warfare Service. Both are West Pointers and Regular Army officers. Another "Armenian" of high rank comes to mind, Colonel Sarkis Zantarian; and I happen to know personally Colonel Emil Antonovich, a construction quartermaster, who is a native San Franciscan of Dalmatian-immigrant parentage. There are hundreds and possibly thousands of other equally "foreign" names in the rapidly expanding Army List, while, as previously suggested, hundreds of thousands of enlisted men answer to such names

as Walzlivick, Tydlacka, Palczak, Reymershoffer, Pustejov-
sky, Jalufka, Serritella, Marimpietri, Giangregorio, Jancso,
Laveccha, Czosnek, Waliszewski, Gryglaszewski, Szyldero-
wicz, Wyndzio, Kolocotronis, Przygodzinski, Blaszka,
Sveinbjornsson, Magnussonar, Arngrimsson, Chukmakjian,
Pasdermajian, Chavira, Chval, Bradarich, Kohlemainen,
Nakamura, Matsuchi, and Bustamantes.

This is from the February 16, 1942, *Time* magazine:
"At Jefferson Barracks, Mo., a roll-calling corporal called
Privates Zlvelachoski, Korczykowski, Svidunovich, and
Squrtieri as best he could."

Essentially the same is true of the Navy. Some of our
most important current and recent admirals are Gherardi,
Taussig, Bloch, Kalbfuss, Nimitz, and Friedel. In other
ranks the Navy List includes such names as Canaga, Bieri,
Gygax, Broshek, Bastedo, Rosendahl, Cohen, Grosskopf,
Ziroli, Vychtlacil, Sallada, Ponto, Botta, Dolecek, Soucek,
Muschlitz, Bagdanovich, Pieczentkowski, Sisko, Kowalzyk,
Zondorak, Durski, Giambattista, Stefanac, Bernstein, Sulz-
berger, Zelenka, Dufek, Tuzo, Dimitrijevic, and Kasparek
—scores and hundreds of them.

It is a fact, however, that the prejudice against "foreigners" in the Navy is greater than in the Army, possibly
because the Navy—like that of England—has always enjoyed more social prestige. It is smaller than the Army, and
is afflicted by "inner cliques" in Washington which are not
altogether free from anti-Semitism, xenophobia, nativism,
and the Social Register. Drew Pearson and Robert S. Allen
in their April 21, 1942, "Washington Merry-Go-Round,"
turned a spotlight on these "brass hats" (their phrase) who

are quietly dishing out commissions and soft berths to scores
of draft eligibles who have the good fortune to be the sons of
rich and influential fathers.

The other day the navy department issued a press release
giving the names of 461 men commissioned as "aviation ad-
ministrative" officers. Between the ages of 27 and 42, they will
hold down desk jobs at induction centers, service schools, etc.

A large percentage of this list of newly made officers are rich young men of the Social Register. These are a few of them:

Colby M. Chester, III, son of the chairman of General Foods Corp.; August Belmont, scion of the famous socialite family; Clifford V. Brokaw, son of a prominent New York broker; Sherman Chickering, son of a leading San Francisco corporation lawyer; Michael Cudahy, of the famous packing family; Herbert Fleischhacker, Jr., son of a San Francisco banker; Channing Frothingham, of a prominent Boston family; Arthur A. Dunn, son of wealthy St. Louis, Mo., realtor; Robert Patterson Jr., and William P. Patterson, of the National Cash Register family; John S. Pillsbury, Jr., son of the Minneapolis flour family; Ogden Phipps of the Long Island Phippses.

Washington is overrun with these young, wealthy socialites who have wangled navy commissions and are fighting the war on the exciting fronts of the capital's embattled cocktail lounges, salons and exclusive clubs. For some reason the Social Registerites seem to prefer the navy. Maybe it's because navy commissions are more easily obtained by the "right people" than army commissions.

This is of course hardly democratic. But it is something that is bound to change as the Navy expands toward the now projected personnel of one million men or over. At least one-third of the already enlisted men are "foreign"-named if I may judge by a list of 1435 promotions to the grade of chief petty officer in the Eleventh Naval District published in the *San Diego Tribune-Sun* of March 31, 1942. It includes such names as these: Abare, Amick, Bacle, Bodnar, Budzilek, Yablonsky, Romanowski, Schwarzin, Swata, Pulezka, Stefanelli, Dauphinais, Stipanovich, Slatsky, Kazezski, Kosturko and Manzuck.

The whole situation in the armed forces will improve too as casualties pile up. Anti-Semitism will dwindle. Early in 1942, when a Gentile soldier introduced to other Gentiles a Jewish friend whom he liked very much, he did not

THE MELTING POT

By special arrangement.

say, "This is Cohen," or ". . . my friend Sam Cohen." He said, "This is Sam." He was trying, perhaps without knowing it, to protect Sam against latent anti-Semitism he felt existed in other Gentiles.

Prejudice against "foreigners" in general will diminish in the Army and Navy as the war develops. One of the boys killed in Hawaii on December 7, 1941, was Peter Niedzwiecki, of Grand Rapids, Michigan; and my guess is that all who know this are already having difficulty in maintaining their prejudice against such names.

Also helpful will be such cartoons as the one from the *Boston Herald*, reproduced on the previous page.

Nonetheless, I think the name problem is sufficiently widespread in the Army and Navy—and also in the Marine Corps—to merit special attention and effort,

Next to the sciences, arts, higher education and snob-appeal luxury trades, "foreign" names rouse least objection in sports, with their philosophy of "fair play" and their occasional international games. Football is particularly free from prejudice, largely owing to the late Knute Rockne, himself a "foreigner." He made famous his formula for estimating the quality of the players his teams were going to meet: "If you can't pronounce them, they're hard to lick." This was half a joke, of course, and parent to the caption "I want you to make Zphgasylzowitch a name to conjure with" that appeared under the drawing of a coach talking to a giant football player in the September 28, 1940, *Saturday Evening Post*. Sports call for more joking and wisecracking than almost any other human activity; and humor, especially the rougher, more obvious sort, if it is not prompted by unkindness or malice, is a great hand at improving relations among simple people. It tackles oversensitiveness and group or personal egoisms as nothing else can.

Humor plays a fine role too in industrial shops. There

*"Happy birthday to you, happy birthday
to you, happy birthday, Tony Matujcyk ..."*

is much good-humored kidding and twisting of unusual appellations into nicknames. These simplifications have a close resemblance to the original jaw-breakers and are then adopted for surnames—another example of fairly organic changing.

The name of the present secretary of the National Association of Die Casting Workers, C.I.O., is Edward T. Cheyfitz. Jacob S. Potofsky is acting president of the Amalgamated Clothing Workers. Most of the other big names in the garment-trade unions in New York are Jewish and Italian, and many district and local officials in some of the new C.I.O. unions have such tags as Damich and Zwaricz. But it appears that—particularly in the steel industry— union leaders with such names have more trouble in obtaining favorable contracts for their men than have leaders with less "un-American"-sounding names. It may be that in some of the industrialists' none-too-well-informed minds a "foreign" name is synonymous with "radicalism," or touches off their Know-Nothing and K.K.K. tendencies.

So it goes. . . .

GIVEN NAMES

In *The American Language,* Mencken devotes a sub-chapter of twenty pages to given names, but, compared with surnames, they are no great problem in the United States; I shall merely touch on the subject.

Non-British new-immigrant families, says Mencken, are downright eager to give "American" first names to their offspring. "The favorite given names of the old country almost disappear in the first native-born generation. The Irish immigrants who flocked in after the famine of 1845-47 bearing such names as Patrick, Terence and Dennis named their American-born sons John, George, William and James. The Germans, in the same way, abandoned Otto, August, Hermann, Ludwig, Rudolf, Heinrich, Wolfgang, Wilhelm, Johann and Franz. For many of these they sub-stituted English equivalents: Lewis, Henry, William, John and Frank, and so on, including Raymond for Raimund."

In a footnote Mencken tells how he came by his own given names. "I was named Henry after my father's brother. Their mother was Harriet McClellan, who came to Baltimore from Kingston, Jamaica. She was of North Irish stock and a member of the Church of England. Henry seems to have been borrowed from some member of her family. I was named Louis after my paternal grandfather, but his actual given names were Burkhart Ludwig. I gather that it was at first proposed to call me Henry Burkhart, but that there was some objection to the Burkhart, probably from my mother. So a compromise was made on Ludwig. Its harsh sound, whether pronounced in the correct Ger-man way or in the American way, caused further qualms, and it was decided to translate it. But the clergyman employed to baptize me wrote it Louis on his certificate, and so I"—a third-generation German American on the male side—"acquired a French name. It was, of course, always pronounced Lewis in the family circle. I have often thought of changing it to something more plausible, but have somehow never got to the business."

In my own case, Louis is even more implausible. In Slovenia as a boy I was first Lojzek, then Lojze (pronounced Loyzek and Loyzé); but I entered the United States with documents made out in my baptismal name, Alojzij (Aloysius). To a few people in New York I continued to be Loyzé for a while, then someone got the notion that "Loyzé" was equivalent to "Louis." I had no objection. I simply became Louis. Some people pronounce the *s*; others leave it silent. Either way is all right with me.

Among Slovenian immigrants, the group I know best, I can think offhand of only seven men of my acquaintance who have been here most of their lives and who still hold onto their original names. I think they retain them partly because they are simple, although some of them can be pronounced more than one way. Four are Ivan, and the others are Janko, Vatro and Anton. But perhaps the more important explanation is that all seven work almost exclusively in cultural and organizational immigrant affairs. Five are editors of Slovenian-language publications, all but one of which are organs of immigrant fraternal societies. The sixth is president of one of these societies and of the Slovenian National Home on St. Clair Avenue in Cleveland, and contributes regularly to several foreign-language papers. The seventh writes poetry in his native language and plays the organ in a Slovenian church.

Some immigrants use both their original and their Americanized first names. I know Slovenian Americans, for instance, who are both Jurij and George, Ivan or Janez and John, Jože and Joe, Francé and Frank. One of my Slovenian American friends in Cleveland finds a peculiar delight in calling me Lojze with a specially strong old-country peasant intonation.

Many Slavic given names are "Americanized" by way of Frenchification. A one-time Andrej I know is André. One of the most active clubwomen in the "Slovenian section" in Cleveland is Mrs. Tončka (or Antonija) Simčič, who is sometimes also Antoinette Simchich.

I know very few second- and third-generation people who haven't "American" first names. In some cases, the middle initial stands for an old-country name. But there seems to be a growing tendency to keep or take on lovely "foreign" first names such as the Scandinavian Ingrid and Sigrid. The former became widely popular in the Northwest after the visit to the United States in 1939 of the Danish Crown Princess Ingrid.

I have a Greek American friend whose children's names are Daphne, Diana, Plato and Spyros.

A considerable number of second- and third-generation Finnish Americans have Finnish first names given at birth or taken on as the group developed pride in their derivation, especially during the 1939-40 Russo-Finnish war to which the American people reacted generally with great admiration for Finland. One Finnish immigrant of my acquaintance has named all his children after heroes and heroines in the Kalevala. This trend probably weakened after Finland joined the Axis.

There is much changing of first names especially by the second generation, both from "foreign" to "American" and the other way about. Some of it is part of the pseudo-nymity business I have discussed. Some is affected by diverse tendencies in altering surnames and to fluctuating notions about what is fashionable. Catherines suddenly become Katrinas. Movie stars influence girls in taking on new given names, which are often "foreign": Greta, Hedy, Marlene, Greer, and so on. Or Fanny Smolnik hears that the daughter of the old-line-American president of the

University of Chicago, Dr. Robert M. Hutchins, is named Franja; so she relabels herself Franja too. A Jewish American woman I know started in life as Sarah; at sixteen she became Shirley; at twenty the Greenwich Village atmosphere in which she lived changed her to Sonia; now she is Sara.

I have already quoted from Mrs. Pearl Cessna Kellogg, a teacher in Fresno County, "than which there is no whicher in the number of new-immigrant groups represented." On the subject of given names she says:

"The 'Americanization' of lovely Armenian names— Agavné, Ardamis, Nevart and Siranoosh into Dovie (!) Diana, Rosie (!) and Hazel moves me almost to tears. To be sure, the teacher is confused by the juxtaposition of Sumiko Kurata and Fumiko Kikuta in the same class, but she nevertheless regrets the recent tendency for all the Sumikos to become Susies and the Fumikos to be known as Fay. Worst of all, Kimiko calls herself Kay, which is after all only a letter in the alphabet."

From other sources, however, I hear that in 1942 many of the Japanese Americans evacuated from the coastal areas of California, Oregon and Washington switched back to Japanese given names: Mary to Mariko, Lillie to Liliko, etc. One youngster said: "Since they insist on considering me a 'Jap,' I may as well have a Jap name!"

WOMEN'S NAMES

HERE and there in this book I have touched on the surname problem as it affects women: "Miss Conrad," "Mrs. Hicks," Miss Svorchek and "Julia Drinkwater." In general, though, women have far less difficulty than men. Most women are expected and want to marry. Widows and divorcees can remarry and thus acquire still another name. In many countries, including the United States, although they may preserve their maiden name as part of their signature, tradition requires them to take on the husband's name, which often holds great significance but is seldom quite as important to them as to the men.

But besides tradition, there may be also this explanation: women have more common sense than men about earthbound reality to which the name question may belong.

On the other hand, as Ambrose Bierce put it, a woman is but "a man with a womb," and in some respects her name problem is the same as man's. Some women, too, have an inner need for independent integrity, for continuous identity under one name. So there are the Lucy Stoners.

Sometimes, though, the Lucy Stone idea doesn't work. For years I have known a married woman of old Yankee stock who went by her maiden name. Let me call her Ann Madison. She is an interesting woman with strong ideas. At one time she was an active feminist. Her immigrant husband was well known in New York and Washington and on the Coast. Let me call him Herbert Leibowitz. He was a brilliant, effective man. He fascinated lots of people including myself. Their city and country homes were almost constantly scenes of stimulating gatherings. Some of the most eminent men and women in America

135

and abroad, Gentiles and Jews, were their friends, many of whom almost never thought of them separately but as "Ann and Herb" or "Herb and Ann." But she was always Ann or Miss Madison, never Mrs. Herbert Leibowitz—except once in a while to a newcomer.

At the height of his career Herb suddenly died in dramatic circumstances. There were long obituaries in the press. Cabinet members, Senators, ambassadors, world-famous philosophers, writers and artists, and many humble folk whom he had helped attended the funeral service. There was never a more mournful widow than Ann Madison.

Only she ceased to be Miss Ann Madison and became Mrs. Herbert Leibowitz. She is now under that name in the telephone directory. Why? I think the Lucy Stoner drowned in her bereft feeling after Herb's death which, though a tragic climax, emphasized the significance of his career and his personal qualities. While he lived, her own name was a symbol of her independence, to which she clung the more insistently the more important he became and the more everybody associated and even identified her with Herb. But when he died she suddenly realized she had had no real existence apart from him. Her own identity as Ann Madison in any vital sense had long since vanished. Now it was pointless to retain her maiden name. To regain her identity, her existence, she took his name which had come to represent them both. The fact that she had been closely associated with him abruptly outweighed the traditional prestige of being Madison. But it may be that more than anything she clings to his name because it is the only part of him left to her.

Of the references to women in the foregoing chapters the case of "Mrs. Hicks" who married to get rid of her Greek name may be the most noteworthy in this connection. I have reason to think that no few second-generation girls of east- and south-European stocks marry "Americans" or men of their own group who have "Americanized" their handles to disburden themselves of their "difficult" Slavic, Greek, Lithuanian, Finnish and Hungarian names. I know at least four young women, one of them divorced, whose choice of a husband was influenced by this consideration, and I suspect it in a number of other cases on which my information is incomplete. The men's "American" names are an attribute which helps the girls to fall in love with them.

SOME LIPPINCOTT MIGHT CHANGE TO
LIPNIKAR

ON THE basis of a rather close examination, I believe that during the next ten or fifteen years all the trends I have discussed will continue to function as elemental manifestations of America's dynamic cultural climate. New trends—some connected with the war and the whole global convulsion—will undoubtedly keep springing up and crisscrossing one another. However, I think the two extreme inorganic tendencies—Anglicization and stubborn resistance to compromise with the English language—are going to weaken, while a strengthening impetus will retain manageable "foreign" names and simplify difficult ones without destroying all trace of their old-country origin.

I have mentioned some reasons for this. There are others. I think it is not unreasonable to expect that many immigrant and second-generation soldiers will distinguish themselves on the far-flung battle fronts of this war. Even if they do not, their service in the American Army, Navy or Marine Corps will tend to integrate them as Americans and make their names American. In one of Rose Feld's charming short stories about "Sophie Halenczik" which have been appearing in *The New Yorker* during 1941-42, Sophie, whose son Frankie is in the Army, gets involved in an affair of the heart with Ernest Hopkins, an elderly and ailing Yankee. It comes to naught, however, partly because:

"Anyway, I don't like the name—Sophie Hopkins. **Nah.** That not me. Sophie Halenczik more better. No?"

"Hopkins is a good old American name," I said.

"Sure," she agreed. "But now Frankie is in the Army, Halenczik is good American name too. No?"

"You bet," I said.

Perhaps a majority of the new-immigrant names are still in, or close to, their original forms. In recent years most of them have been recorded in the Social Security, Selective Military Service, Alien Registration files, rationing and numerous other records, and a change will now involve much red tape—something many foreign-born and second-generation people try to avoid even more than most old-stock Americans. A sense of inferiority and unfamiliarity holds them away from any unnecessary contact with the government. To be sure this will also retard the tendency toward simplification, but less so than toward Anglicization. It probably will not much affect the dropping of consonants in very difficult names.

Other ways of dealing with names are apt to develop. *Who's Who in America* has begun to give pronunciations of some of the "foreign" names. The educational departments of several large new-immigrant fraternal-insurance organizations have published in English and distributed to schools, libraries and social agencies rules of pronunciation for the tough names in their groups. In 1939 the "Nationalities Division" of the Detroit Council of Social Agencies issued a list of rules on Polish names. And some people who retain their names add the pronunciation in parentheses on business cards and stationery. Federal Reserve Board Governor Menc Stephen Szymczak (Simchek) does this.

As already suggested, I do not favor changing names even with an alternative pronunciation simply because they are non-English. Tabor, Bokor, Svorchek, Sitoski, Badura, Kunefko, Kolssack, Piontek, Kudlick, Nowak, Bogin, Miksa, Farkas, Hika, Lopilato, Palumbo, Gogolin, Soluk, Montefinese, Bakjian, Maksymyk and Skouras are no more troublesome than Abernethy, which is pronounced one way in the South and another in the North, or Featherstoneleigh, which is found in the South and elsewhere. It should be borne in mind that Americans in general have not yet made up their minds as to the pronunciation of "Roosevelt" and of many place names, although there have been two President Roosevelts and the places have been here for a long time. New Orleans for instance has at least three variations and St. Louis at least two. Arkansas is pronounced one way for the state, another for the river. Miami is Miami to some people, Miamer to others. Houston is Hews-ton in Texas and House-ton in many other places. Tivoli is simple enough, but Texans say it Tievoh'ler. Even many ordinary words are pronounced one way in New York, another in Vermont, and differently still in the South, in Oregon, and in Arizona.

In the paragraph immediately preceding I listed "Maksymyk," the name of a Ukrainian-American family living in Lancaster, New York, which in 1942 had four sons in the Army. Who would say that theirs is not an American name and would require them to change it? Hasn't the rest of the country an obligation to learn to pronounce it with ease? It really is no harder, say, than Gildersleeve or MacInnes. Or take Kalakuka; it is the name of a lieutenant colonel of Ukrainian descent who was decorated in May, 1942, for "heroism beyond the line of duty" while fighting on the Island of Cebu. I suggest he be allowed to keep it.

But, as also indicated, I do favor simplification of really difficult names and I do not object to adjusting even the not-so-difficult ones, such as my own. Personally, I am perfectly willing to learn how to pronounce and spell Krzyzanowski, Cachazounian, Demetracopoulos, Dvaranskas, Kopankiewicz, Przybylowicz, Szczypiorski, and Runovaara. But immigrants and the second generation whose disposition is to resist emendation at all costs might consider that such names are Polish, Armenian, Greek, Lithuanian and Finnish whereas their bearers now inhabit the United States, a country considerably unlike Poland, Armenia, Greece, Lithuania or Finland. As people, they are therefore considerably different from what they would be if they had remained in the Old World. In other words, they are no longer Poles, Armenians, Greeks, Lithuanians and Finns. Technicalities aside, if they have lived here long enough they are Americans—Polish, Armenian, Greek, Lithuanian or Finnish Americans, but conclusively Americans, however they may differ from the old stock. It could be argued that, as Americans, if their names are manageable only by those who know the old-country tongues, they are probably a little misnamed. After all, the language of the United States *is* English—a fact which nobody disputes.

This is so ticklish a subject with so many people, it is so shot through with emotion and natural unreasonableness, that I feel the need of emphasizing that I am not dogmatic. I merely urge new-immigrant people to consider the facts, and I suggest it would be wise to adjust their names to fit with their status as new-stock Americans. It would be particularly sensible where their fellow Americans of other strains find their names awkward or difficult. A good many people simply lack the time to acquaint themselves with the pronunciation and orthography of a dozen or more languages which are radically different from English. Some people whose speech organs have been formed by the use of English cannot ever master the pronunciation of many "foreign" names no matter how hard they try.

And I suggest, too, if one decides to modify his name he bear in mind that American speech, as already hinted, has a predilection for accenting the first or second syllable. Let the name be simplified with some regard for what it will look like on paper and how it will sound. Let there be a little consideration for the average teacher, mailman, storekeeper, library clerk and registrar who will have to fit it into his spelling and pronunciation habits.

Let there be some regard for euphony. Some years ago Leonard Feeney, one of the editors of the Catholic weekly, *America,* wrote an article on this subject, which was then condensed in *The Literary Digest.* "The most frightening name I have heard," he said, "is Edmund Blunden; the most friendly Laura Benét." He shuddered at the lack of euphony in his own name, and listed the following:

Ugly names: Negley Farson, Avery Brundage, Aldous Huxley and Westbrook Pegler.

Singsong names: Fanny Burney, Percy Bysshe Shelley, Eugene O'Neill.

Unsuccessful combinations: James Joyce, John Keats, Sol Blum.

Successful combinations: Alexander Pope, Lafcadio Hearn, Christopher Wren, John Galsworthy, Jacques Maritain.

From the unsuccessful and the successful combinations Leonard Feeney concluded that two monosyllabic names should be buttressed by a polysyllabic one: George Bernard Shaw, John Bannister Tabb, James Montgomery Flagg, etc. He begged that in naming babies parents select tags which "will give a child a fighting chance—or relieve him of an adolescent obligation to fight," and the *Digest* offered the following suggestions on "How To Name Baby":

1. If the surname has one syllable, avoid a one-syllable first name. Example: Montgomery Smith rather than George or John Smith.

2. With a two-syllable last name, use either a one-syllable or three-syllable Christian name. Example: John Hinton or Christopher Hinton rather than William Hinton or Frederick Hinton.

3. When the last name has three syllables, use either a one- or two-syllable first name. Example: Mary Dougherty or George Dougherty, but not Alexander Dougherty.

4. If a middle name is to be used, it should contain more or fewer syllables than the surname, never the same.

5. Avoid overlapping consonants such as Kathleen Norris, Bernard De Voto, or James Stephens.

6. Get away as much as possible from John, Albert, Elsie and Alice. In later life men sometimes feel John is too common a name. Albert briefs into an undignified nickname. Elsie and Alice sound "arty" enough to cause discomfort.

What's in a name? "Plenty!" answered an editorial writer in the July 9, 1932, New York *World-Telegram*. "The name makes or breaks the man. The sound of it, beginning life with its owner and going along with him, certainly has some influence in the shaping of his personality." The name is certainly likely to shape the public attitude toward the person, and the writer continued:

Thomas W. Wilson (Woodrow) saw that.

Hiram S. Grant became Ulysses.

Herbert Blythe turned into Maurice Barrymore, sire of the "Royal Family."

Names are bound to mean something when a mere calling off of those of the prominent figures in the world today shows almost invariably some distinctiveness which catches the ear and eye and lingers.

Mussolini, Gandhi, Stalin, Einstein, G. B. Shaw, Hamsun, Rockefeller, Lindbergh, Borah, La Follette, Paderewski, Jeritza, Lily Pons, Tunney, "Babe" Ruth, Capone, "Alfalfa Bill." Could these men and women have gone as far with undistinctive names?

Clearly the inequalities of life attach to the names people inherit or acquire or assume, as well as to wealth or rank.

Perhaps much of this needs to be considered in giving and changing names.

And, most important, new-immigrant folk should struggle against mere defensiveness within themselves; it is ruinous to character and at the least leads to all sorts of contretemps. They should question whether they hang onto their "difficult" names because of the primitive motives and impulses I have suggested. Others need to find out if they are name or man. New-immigrant people should do a good deal of thinking about their place in America and America's future. Considerateness will then follow almost as a matter of course. It is no slight virtue in a democracy. It is a prerequisite for the give-and-take of everyday life.

Of course, it takes more than one side to give and take. Old-stock Americans should curb their impatience with unfamiliar names, as should new-immigrant folk with names belonging to people of other backgrounds than their own. There should be no insistence upon Anglicization; it only drives new-stock groups and individuals into an unhealthy self-defense. It is integral with the unsound if not dangerous illusion and pretense that the United States is completely Anglo-Saxon—that old-line Americans constitute the standard national type. Why should Tarpidatitulian be forced to overhaul himself into Turner to prove his Americanism? If he consents to change, why not to Tarpidian or Tarpian?

But the important thing to remember is that one becomes an American by learning to participate in and contribute to American life. The process is both a drawing and a giving of strength. Integration with this country is not determined by an Anglo-Saxon name.

I think that a new type of human being is evolving in America, an amalgam of many strains and cultures. I hope so. It will not be an Anglo-Saxon type, nor Polish, nor German, nor Bulgarian. It will be American. And the Americans of the future will have names derived from many nations. They will be not particularly English, Scottish, Polish, German or Czech. They will be American.

Also, we need to realize that after the current war the United States is likely to get into close relationship with many nations. Those peoples have "foreign" names which we Americans will have to respect and learn how to pronounce. We may even have to get used to Chakravarthi Rajagopalachariar ("C. R."), the name of one of the Indian leaders. Unless we begin to respect the "foreign" names at home, we are sure to have difficulties abroad, later. Respecting them, we are apt to be taking a step toward developing the world-mindedness more and more clearly required of us by the immense predicament in which America is involved.

However, this is a long way ahead. Right now we all need a little perspective on the names situation as a whole. Few individuals are able to acquire it by themselves. As I have suggested, it will be necessary for schools, settlement houses, churches, service and cultural clubs, the Army and Navy and many other organizations and institutions to help.

I must repeat that I favor *organic* changing of names, such as occurred with mine or with that of my friend George A. Elmott, an American veteran of the First World War now living in California.

His parents brought George to the United States from Ruthenia when he was seven. The family name was Ehnot. His father died, and a few years later his mother remarried and all the children by her first husband were renamed Biletz. "Then," George told me thirty-five years later, "I saw an ad in a magazine which said 'Be yourself! Give yourself a chance! You, too, can be popular! Send for our Steel Guitar and Five Free Lessons for only $2.98.' It sounded swell, so I wrote to the advertiser. One idea I had about being myself was to sign my right name —Ehnot. But the reply came addressed: George Elmott. Somehow in being hand-written, the little doodad forming the lower part of the *h* got carried over to the *n*, which made the *h* an *l*, and the *n* an *m*; while the extra *t*, I suppose, was put on to balance the name. . . . Why not be

Elmott? I had no objection. And so when the United States went to war I enlisted under that name.

"I had a buddy in the Army who had lots of talent for asking questions. After the Armistice we marched through Belgium to Germany. In camp one night, he asked if I had a middle name: the sort of question this fellow was liable to ask anybody any time. I said no. Why not? I said I never thought I needed one. Hell's bells, he said, a man's got to have a middle name. It turned out that he hadn't one, either, which made him feel very low. Then he said, 'Say, George, let's you and me both take the name of this town we're in for our middle name. It's Arlon; it sounds fine; it'll be a kind of war souvenir.' I said okay, and I've been George Arlon Elmott ever since. . . ."

I find no Elmotts in the telephone books of a number of large American cities. So far as I know, there are no Elmotts anywhere else in the world. The name seems to me a new American name, which came into existence organically in the United States. It sounds all right.

Of course George is a fortunate fellow. What happened to his name was not of any consequence to him. He was never his name. He was always first of all a person. His inner make-up is equipped with all sorts of philosophical and psychological devices which overcome with wisecracks such petty inferiorities as assail him. He has no permanent defenses; he needs none. He is what he is. He has to have a name; what difference does it make what it is so long as it's easy to use? In short, George A. Elmott comes close to being a hint of the new type of American with a new-American name.

I own a little farm on the Jersey side of the Delaware Valley. My nearest neighbor is a farmer named Phil Lippincott. The man who does most of the work on my place is an elderly immigrant from Slovenia, Andy Krizmančič, whose English is no great shakes. The two men are good

friends. But Andy's old Slovenian tongue can't manipulate "Lippincott" so he calls our neighbor Lipnikar, which
is a common handle in Slovenia, meaning "Lindenman";
while Phil, equally helpless about "Krizmančič," addresses
him as Kriz. For a time they tried to get each other to
pronounce their names "correctly," then gave it up as
hopeless. Now they are simply Kriz and Lipnikar. Of
course neither will change his name. Both are along in
years. Krizmančič and Lippincott are the names that belong to them and to some extent they are their names.
Lippincott's young boy Johnny, though, is different. He
likes Kriz to call him Tchonny Lipnikar. He has tried to
give Lipnikar as his name in school. He thinks it is "nicer"
than Lippincott. It sounds better to him. It is two letters
shorter and easier to spell.

I don't suppose Johnny will eventually rename himself
Lipnikar. But the lad has given me an amusing idea. Lipnikar may be really simpler, and to some it may sound
better than Lippincott; so why shouldn't some Lippincott
one day change to Lipnikar? No doubt some Slovenian
immigrant originally named Lipnikar has already taken
on Lippincott.

If a few Lippincotts changed to Lipnikar or Lipinski
and if one or two "real" New England Cabots turned
Kobotchnik, they would be front-page news. Radio news-
men would talk about them. Editorial writers would go to
town. A few of them published editorials when, early in
1942, one John Doe Smith, of San Diego, legally changed to
John Joseph Banducci.

Such an extreme reversal would not in itself of course
end the great American battle of names. But it would cast
a new and startling light. It would emphasize many of the
aspects I have mentioned. It might help bring about an
emotional as well as an intellectual understanding of the
problem of "foreign" names which now bedevils millions
of Americans.

Alias Mr. Nichols

A Narrative

All the personal and most of the place names in this story are disguised, along with some situations. I place the high school where "Mr. Nichols" taught in Cleveland, but —let me emphasize—it need not be assumed that Cleveland is the city. Nor that the material came to me as I present it.

L. A.

It is a strange thing—to be an American—
America is neither a land nor a people.
A world's shape it is, and a wind's sweep—
America is alone: many together. . . .

—ARCHIBALD MACLEISH

MR. NICHOLS WANTS TO TELL ME ABOUT
HIMSELF

One evening early in 1939 I spoke before an audience in Cleveland. "Plymouth Rock and Ellis Island" was the title of my talk. It concerned developments in American life rising out of the arrival in the United States during the past hundred years of nearly forty million immigrants representing close to threescore national and religious backgrounds and several distinct races.

I held that these developments, some extremely subtle, contained large possibilities, good and bad, for the country's future, and also many difficulties for millions of individuals belonging to new-immigrant and old-stock groups. Among other difficulties I mentioned those connected with "foreign" names.

After the talk a slight, neatly dressed young man in his middle thirties came up and introduced himself as John Nichols. He said he was a high-school teacher and would like to talk to me.

I asked him to come to my hotel.

When he entered my room and I took his coat and hat, he said, "I told you my name is Nichols. It *is*, in a way— John S. Nichols. Legally that is my name; but it wasn't always. My middle initial stands for the one I started with—Sobuchanowsky." He smiled uneasily.

I said I assumed he was American-born.

He replied that he was, and sat down. He clasped his hands, then quickly unclasped them. It was as though he suddenly remembered he had determined to appear calm and matter-of-fact while talking to me. But this explanation only occurred to me much later when he had told me most of his story.

"While you were talking about troubles with 'foreign' names," he said, "I decided—on an impulse—that I would try to see you. I'd like to tell you about my difficulty if you have the time and patience to listen to me."

A LEMKO IMMIGRANT AND HIS YOUNG
CHILDREN

Mr. Nichols began at the beginning:

"My father, Nikolai Sobuchanowsky, emigrated to America in 1903. He came from somewhere in the Carpathian Mountains. I don't know the name of the village. Before 1918 it was in Austria; then it was included in Poland or Czechoslovakia, I don't know which. It doesn't really matter.

"In the old country my father belonged to a little-known nationality—the Lemkoes. These people seem to be concentrated between the San and Poprad rivers. They are a small nation, if they are a nation; perhaps they are just a branch of the Ukrainian people. At least that is what some Ukrainians claim. Most Lemkoes are themselves uncertain whether they are Ukrainians, Russians or Poles, or merely Lemkoes. My father doesn't know to this day. He doesn't care. Russian, Ukrainian, Pole, or Lemko—it's all the same to him.

"The Lemkoes have a confused religious status. Their traditional church is a combination of the Greek Orthodox rite and the Roman Catholic dogma and discipline. It is called the Uniate Church. But many Lemkoes in Poland and Slovakia are now 'real' Catholics; while in places where the old-time Russian Church was a strong influence a lot of them became Orthodox. I am not sure what my father was in the old country but I think he came from a Uniate village.

"When he came to America, he went to Dexter, a soft-coal town in southwestern Pennsylvania, where other Lemkoes, including a cousin of his, had gone to work in the mines. Dad became a miner too.

"He was a small, thin man. Back in his native country he had not had very much to eat. He never weighed much over a hundred pounds. He had short bow-legs and long arms and big hands. He was all bone and skin and sinew, disproportionately powerful for his size, and the mine bosses considered him a good worker.

"Nobody bothered to remember his surname; they all called him Nick.

"Dad and Mother first became interested in each other one Sunday at the home of a fellow countryman in Dexter. I suppose it was a typical Sunday afternoon gathering of Slavic immigrant miners. There was drinking, eating, music, dancing and boasting about how much they had earned the last two weeks, or about the size of the lumps of coal they had broken off the vein, or how deep underground they worked.

"Mother too was from the Carpathians but had come to America as a girl of twelve. Now she was seventeen. Her father, also a Lemko, was employed in the same mine as Dad and thought him an acceptable son-in-law—he never missed a shift.

"They married in 1904. I imagine Mother quickly regretted it. She did not have a good life. She bore seven children in less than eight years. I am the oldest. There was a girl before me who died in infancy. Later a two-year-old brother was killed by a train as he crawled over the rails after a kitten. We lived by the tracks. Long trains of coal cars passed our house every hour or so. I remember that in summer when we had our windows open the engines belched smoke and fine hot cinders into the rooms.

"Another brother of mine died of a sudden illness, also in early childhood. Mother woke me one morning and said, 'Nikolai is dead.'

"My recollections of Mother are dim. But one fact sticks hard in my mind: she was often cross with us children. Not that I blame her. She and Dad were not a very good match—though it may be bad taste to say a thing like this about one's parents. She had gone to the public school in Dexter for two or three years and spoke fairly good English. She considered herself 'Americanized' and wanted to wear nice clothes and go out and be gay, while Dad had a different idea of life.

"He was what the Scotch-Irish and Welsh bosses in town called 'just a Hunky'—all work, work, and more work. But this by no means describes him; the 'Americans' never really understood the 'Hunkies.' A few years ago in a sudden soft moment Dad told me how he had felt when he first saw the Statue of Liberty. 'I cry like hell,' he said. . . .

"Dad liked America from the start even if he never showed it and always looked harried, desperate and tired. His idea was to work hard, earn as much money as you could and spend no more than you absolutely had to and save the rest. It was an obsession with him. He knew he was face-to-face with a tough proposition. Some of this he had doubtless brought with him from the old country, where poverty was the chief note of peasant existence. The rest he developed here working at a dangerous job below-earth and living in a strange country full of baffling phenomena.

"Father handled all the money himself, did all the shopping and even collected from the boarders. Mother never had more than a quarter in the house. Dad made her keep a boardinghouse, and she cooked and washed for a dozen men as well as her own family. Childbearing was incidental, a brief annual interruption of her routine. An interlude. Her life was no joke; at twenty-three or -four her looks were gone. Every once in a while she rebelled. There were nasty scenes. Once I remember she tried to smash Dad over the head with a chair. He ducked just in time, then hit her. And I seem to have heard that still earlier she had tried to leave him and go off with one of the boarders. He went after her and brought her back.

"I am trying to tell you the truth about my father and mother; but I don't want to give you a wrong impression, especially of Dad. I'm eager you should not think ill of him. In his queer 'Hunky' way he has been a good man, even a mild, gentle man; only he seldom would show the best in him. He is a peasant, which probably covers him in a nutshell. Years ago I read Reymont's novel, *The Peasants,* and I suspect there is no such thing as a 'simple peasant.' I wouldn't be surprised if there is no human being more complicated and twisted. In addition to what I have already told you about my father, I should probably explain that Dad was so tight in money matters because he wanted security for his family. In those days for a man in his situation there was no security apart from what he earned and saved. He might be crippled or killed; then where would his family be? . . .

"Dad was hardest with himself. He drove himself or something inside him drove him like a slave. I don't pretend to understand him really. All I am sure of are certain facts about his behavior and some glimpses of his inner make-up that I have caught off and on during the years.

"At any rate this went on for eight years. Then Mother fell ill and died. Pneumonia. She was up one day working, yelling at us; dead the next. The last baby was only a few months old. I was barely seven.

"Mother's death was a great blow to Dad. He went in back of the culm pile which loomed like a mountain across the tracks from our house, and wept. He roared like a stuck ox. I saw him go and followed him. There he sat on a big piece of slag holding his head in his hands—and that awful sound coming out of him! I suppose he loved Mother, maybe so deep-down, so twistedly, so like a peasant, that his real feeling for her came out only now. While she lived, so far as I can recall, he had shown her no consideration, no tenderness. Perhaps now he was sorry; I don't know.

"When he saw me he almost physically gulped down his grief. He stopped crying, wiped his face on his sleeve, rose and without saying a word took my hand and led me back to the house.

"He had never taken my hand like this before.

"So now, here was this man, my father, with four young children on his hands. Except for the funeral he was afraid to miss a single day's work. As before, he went off at five-thirty every morning and returned at five-thirty in the afternoon. He worked ten hours a day. There was an hour for lunch and it took him about half an hour to get to the mine.

"A young unmarried sister of Mother's came over to do the housekeeping, but she was no match for the situation. One by one the boarders left. Mike and Joe, the two youngest children, cried most of the time. Our young aunt did not know what to do with them. My sister Annie, next to me in age, was only six. I began to go to school and probably was the most wretched of us all.

"Although I was a native American my English was very poor. Nearly all the talk I had heard was Ukrainian or Russian. Only Mother had burst occasionally into English —as if in protest against her predicament. And to Miss Watkins, my first-grade teacher, I was one of 'those foreign kids' with an unpronounceable name, a two-legged problem and nuisance. Whenever I happened to come within range of her eyes she grimaced. Most of the time she tried to ignore me along with the other 'foreign children.' I was afraid of her and, probably more because of this than on account of my poor English, understood almost nothing she said. Sometimes it was all I could do to keep from breaking into tears in the middle of a lesson. Also, my clothes were worse than the other children's. They were crude and too big. Dad bought everything we wore without taking us along. He went on the theory that size was unimportant. Suppose they were too large! We would grow. I remember my shoes were always much too big no matter how tightly I laced them. . . .

"When most of the boarders had left, and Dad realized that our aunt would not do for the mistress of his household, he gave up the big ramshackle frame house by the tracks . . . and for a time we lived in various Ukrainian boardinghouses where we children were a nuisance to the grownups. They stumbled over us, stepped on us in the dark, pushed us around and cursed us.

"This was probably the worst period in my life. As I talk to you I seem to be pulling the facts out of a gray fog.

"We moved three or four times, each time to a more chaotic place. There were brawls, sudden outbursts of ignorance and poverty. The women running the boardinghouses were too busy with their own children and their regular boarders to bother with us. They fed us, then literally locked us up out of the way.

"At night we slept or lay restlessly awake wherever there happened to be a spot to curl up in: in crates under the sink, on top of the basket full of dirty clothes or in a corner on the floor. In the last boardinghouse we had a little privacy. Dad, Mike and I slept together on a wide bed, Annie on a torn mattress spread on the floor and Joe, the baby, in a rusty old wash boiler beside her. He ailed a great deal and cried most of the time.

"Gradually it dawned on Dad that this would not do in the long run either. I imagine that in spite of his less attractive characteristics he could easily have remarried. He was a terrific, steady worker, and the Ukrainian and Russian widows in town whose husbands had died in the mines no doubt eyed him speculatively. But he decided against it—God knows by what instinct or process of reasoning. He might really have been in love with Mother.

"Somehow, perhaps through a translator, he communicated the nature and intensity of his problem to the mine bosses who were sympathetic. They transferred him to the night shift and after he learned to operate the pump they put him in charge of getting water out of the pits. For Dad this had the additional advantage of being a steady job. He worked whether the miners worked or not—the water had to be pumped up—and he has been at it ever since. He is now in his sixties. . . .

"Then we moved into a house by ourselves again. It was a lopsided, unpainted little place near both the mine and the school. Dad paid seven dollars a month rent and maybe it wasn't worth that, but it was a tremendous improvement over the boardinghouses.

"Dad left the house at quarter to six every evening, Sundays included; and he quit work at five the next morning. He usually was so tired he could barely drag himself home. We were still in bed when he came, and before we got up he made a fire and prepared breakfast.

"Sometimes when I came down at six or six-thirty, unable to sleep because I had heard him puttering around and felt sorry for him, I found the stove going with everything ready for us, and my father sprawled out in deep slumber on the landing. Then Annie would come down too pulling Mike after her; and occasionally we had to pinch Dad's hands or pull his mustache to wake him up so he could have his breakfast and go to bed.

"He slept till one or two in the afternoon, then went shopping. About three-thirty he began to cook supper. Before he left the house, winter or summer, he made us all go to bed. There was no arguing with him on this point. Or on any other point. He was an utter tyrant. We lived in a state of continuous emergency; and so far as Dad could see there were no two ways of handling it. He held Annie responsible for Joe, me for Mike.

"We had no electricity and Dad forbade us to light a candle or a lamp. In fact I think that for some years we had neither in the house. The matchbox was hidden out of our reach. But even so, working at his pump, he worried about us. Twenty years later he confessed to me—in an offhand joke—that during his lunch period at midnight he had often run home to make sure we were all right. He unlocked the door quietly, came in, listened, then ran back to his job. Annie and I never heard him.

"With a few important changes, which I shall tell you about, this went on for seven solid years. Dad was never affectionate and was often gruff in a tired, harried, frantic way. Apart from his orders, warnings and threats before he left the house he seldom said anything to us. He never bought us any presents, only what we needed. He fed us amply but only the cheapest food. His entire expenses for rent, clothing and groceries probably did not exceed thirty-five dollars a month. He saved the rest . . . and I believe that by the time I was fourteen he was worth three thousand dollars or more. The money was all put away for the future in case he suddenly died in the mine or something.

"Today Dad is a kind of hero to me; even as a small boy I dimly perceived his role in this 'gray period.' But when I was seven and eight I half-hated him because he was my father and I was his child and had to live in those boardinghouses and later in that shack by ourselves, and I was a 'foreign kid,' a 'Hunky' named Johnny Sobuchanowsky who could not speak good English; all of which made life in school miserable for me.

"Miss Watkins may have been all right for the 'American' children—in so far as she was interested in teaching at all. It was probably only temporary to her. She was not a bad woman but just more or less anti-'foreign'—'foreign' meaning the Slavic, Italian, Greek and Lithuanian nation-alities in town. She had other things on her mind and it was easier for her to be anti-'foreign' than to understand the new people and do something to make them feel and act less alien. She certainly was not in the least helpful to us 'foreign kids.'

"The principal, who was Scotch-Irish of four or five generations in America, was no better from my angle than Miss Watkins. When some of us 'foreign' pupils were not passed to the second grade he came to class and called our names, stumbling and grinning over each of them and saying things to us. Most of us were not sure what he meant. Some of the 'American' kids giggled. The principal had a lot of difficulty over my name and made me pro-nounce it two or three times: *Sobuchanowsky, Sobu-chanowsky.* My voice sounded like thunder in my ears. My mouth and throat were dry. I wanted to run away.

"We were still living in our last boardinghouse, and when I saw Dad that evening I could not look at him. I wanted to throw something at him. I ate no supper; I went out and hid behind the fence of a vacant old house and cried. I told myself I was dumb because I was a 'foreigner,' because that skinny, goofy-looking guy Nick Sobuchanow-sky was my old man. . . .

"The following year Annie started going to school. By then we had established ourselves in the little house. Dad was asleep when we left home, and we locked up the two younger kids in a bare room next to him where they could not hurt themselves and he would hear them if they cried. Mike was five and getting to be a quiet dependable lad.

"Annie and I were both in the first grade because I had failed. For a while she was even more sensitive about being a 'foreigner' than I. That year the majority of the class was 'foreign' and Miss Watkins was beside herself. On the first day of school she sent the two of us home because we were dirty or our clothes were torn; I forget which. Some of the other children laughed at us and Annie was so humiliated she sobbed all the way home.

"We woke Dad up and he got mad. He leaned on his elbows in bed and glared at us. What time was it? What were we doing home? Annie told him, while I noticed how dirty his shirt was. He raged at us and our teacher. These crazy Americans! Suppose something was a little dirty or torn! He could not see that clothes had any other purpose than to cover your nakedness and keep you from freezing.

"I don't remember how the issue resolved itself that morning. Eventually Annie and I developed a knack of being cleaner and neater in spite of Dad.

"We were embarrassed too over the huge sandwiches Dad made for us to take to school. They were the same size as the ones he put into his own lunch-bucket: a quarter-of-an-inch-thick piece of boloney between two large slices of bread. He put the sandwiches—one apiece—in a paper bag for us, and Annie and I used to hide them. At noon we sneaked behind the building where no one could see us, and we devoured them as quickly as possible.

"The sandwiches which the 'American' children ate were small and neat, and each youngster had two or three wrapped separately in paper. They were ham, cheese, egg, and beef sandwiches, not just boloney. Sometimes the crust was cut away around the bread, which was also buttered or smeared with 'that green-yellow stuff,' as Annie and I used to call mustard before we knew what it was.

"The 'American' children had cakes, cookies, apples, bananas and oranges. Dad did not believe in any such fancy food. To him food was to fill the stomach, to keep you in strength, and you could accomplish that with most food if you had enough of it. And so the sensible thing to do was to eat the things you got most of for your money.

Quantity, bulk was what counted. Boloney cost only a few cents a pound.

"We almost never had any fruit although in the summertime it must have been very cheap. Once a girl named Esther Thomas, the daughter of a mine superintendent, offered me her apple. I wanted it terribly (and I worshiped her for a long time afterward) but I was so timid I declined it.

"Annie and I tried to tell Dad about our sandwiches. We got nowhere; he was a veritable mule when it came to progress of this sort. At such moments our regard for him became all mixed up with an almost murderous hate. We were too young to be objective and see that with his old-country peasant heritage and in his isolation he was not in a position to realize what school was like.

"But presently Annie learned how to get around him. She told him she could fix our lunch herself and after a while he let her do it. She offered, too, to get up early and make breakfast before he came home but he would not let her; it would have meant spending a dollar for an alarm-clock. Also, children require a lot of sleep. This notion he probably brought from the old country—part of his small fund of wisdom.

"Dad never saw us off to school; he was snoring away by then; so we could scrub our faces, necks and ears daily, and dress neatly. When we got home in the afternoon we mussed ourselves up a little and changed to old clothes which we hid from Dad in the daytime. He could not keep in his mind a complete inventory of our small wardrobe.

"In other words, Annie and I were practically subversive. It was the only way to circumvent our father's tyranny and backwardness.

"A word more about our school sandwiches. Annie fixed them, when Dad had gone upstairs after breakfast, in imitation of those we saw the well-to-do 'American' youngsters eat. We had no cheese or ham, but she fried eggs and put them between thin slices of bread. Or she made sandwiches of the scraps of pork left over from supper. And she cut off the crust. It was not thrown away, however; we munched it on the way to school.

"So began our Americanization.

"MEEZ MEEF"

"Then came a lucky break. That fall our old principal left, and during the winter Miss Watkins quit. I never heard of her again. I felt an immense relief when she was gone.

"For a couple of days we had no teacher.

"Then Miss Mifflin appeared. She was a thin middle-aged little woman with kind eyes and a nice smile. She was all sincerity; her manner accepted you, took you in. All of us 'foreign kids' knew at once we would not have to be afraid of her. The first day we had her Annie and I bubbled all the way home.

"For my part even then, Miss Mifflin was old-time America at its best. She was a fine teacher and all goodness as a person. Where she came from or why she had landed in Dexter I don't know, but she became an influence for good in our school. She seemed to know the new principal well; and we heard that she talked to other teachers who were impatient with the 'Ukrainian,' 'Polack,' 'Slovak' and 'Italian' children. She believed a teacher should have the same pupils as long as possible, and the principal let her take us all the way up to the sixth grade.

"Miss Mifflin lifted a cloud from my mind. When she first came to my name she asked me how I pronounced it. I shook all over but managed to tell her how I heard it at home. She said it had a very interesting sound. Then she always spoke it carefully: So-bu-cha-now-sky. She was of course just as considerate of other 'foreign' youngsters, and most of us ceased to feel strange. A kind of glow spread over me every time she showed me something in my reader or took hold of my hand to help me with my penmanship, and I realized that if I tried hard my work would earn recognition; I might even be praised. It was all I needed. Suddenly I felt quite at home in English as though I had known it all the time and Miss Mifflin had merely removed a barrier. In the second grade I rose to the top of the class . . . and remained above-average through the rest of my formal education.

"Our new teacher was interested in us as people. Pretty soon she noticed that Annie and I never had any fruit for lunch. She asked us about it and Annie told her our father was 'funny' that way. We had no mother? No. I elaborated a little, and after school Miss Mifflin asked if she might walk home with us. She encouraged us to tell her our story. She studied us. She stopped us and looked behind our eyelids and at our teeth. Did we ever have a toothache. No. Were we ever sick? And so on. Finally she asked us to see if she might pay Dad a visit the following day.

"Dad was all flustered at first. What did she want? We said she was very nice to us and wanted to meet him. What for? I said I didn't know. Annie had no idea either. These Americans! In the end he said all right.

"When Miss Mifflin came, Dad was beside himself. He had put the house in as good order as he knew how, and still looked around—frantically, furtively—to see if he could not improve the downstairs room which was vestibule, kitchen, dining- and living-room, all in one. On the table was a plate; on the plate, lo and behold! were several apples and an orange.

"Annie and I looked at the fruit, then at one another, then at Miss Mifflin. She saw at once that he had bought it to brighten up the room; and she commented upon its color.

"Apart from mining terms Dad still spoke very little English and he grinned at Miss Mifflin like an idiot. Annie and I were terribly embarrassed. But gradually Miss

Mifflin's manner put him at ease. She was natural and direct; there wasn't a trace of condescension about her. Dad listened and tried to understand or let us translate what she was saying. She said fruit was healthy and children ought to eat some everyday. 'An apple a day,' she quoted, 'keeps the doctor away.'

"Dad pondered, then looked at her and nodded emphatically: 'Sure! Goot!'

"After this we had fruit daily; Dad even treated himself now and then.

"For Miss Mifflin's first visit Dad had locked Mike and Joe, now about three, in their 'prison' upstairs. Miss Mifflin asked about them and Annie brought them down. They were scrubbed clean and fairly neatly dressed. Not used to strangers, they backed away from Miss Mifflin and Joe started to wail. Dad made a sudden move to shut him up but Miss Mifflin got between them, picked up Joe and quieted him in a minute.

"The upshot of that afternoon was that Dad developed a great respect for 'Meez Meef' and she a special interest in our family. She might have become endlessly involved with us had her health not been uncertain. Obliged to watch her limited energy, she curbed her impulse to help us at nearly every turn.

"Even so she came to the house about once a week for more than five years and she always brought us a nickel's worth of raisins or peanuts. In Dad's eyes everything she did was right. He followed her advice and let her show him and Annie how to improve their cooking. She criticized our clothes and brought him around to taking us shopping with him.

"How to explain her? I suppose our being motherless touched her. There is no question but that we were a pathetic crew. Dad at once disturbed her and commanded her respect. She wanted to help him although I imagine mostly for our sake. She realized that we were none too firm and clear in our feeling toward Dad and she may have suspected that at times we hated him. So she frequently spoke of him in terms of admiration—a few times in his presence, which spread wide grins over his face and heightened his tendency to revere the ground she walked on.

"He did not do quite everything she wanted. She tried to get him to become an American citizen, and he was willing until he saw what it involved. He maintained he could not learn 'a goot Ehngleesh' because he was 'soo doomb.' His job ruled out night school; besides, since he was 'doomb' it would be useless to try to teach him. And also, peasant-like, he was always afraid of going through any kind of official procedure. Miss Mifflin let the matter drop. I suspect she did not consider citizenship terribly important for him.

"But through the five years of our friendship she directed at him an intensive campaign to make him realize that his children were Americans. We were all quite bright and Miss Mifflin made Dad very proud of that. She planted the idea in him that nothing was too good for us. We were Americans, she said to him over and over again, and he should see we had the same opportunities as other young Americans. He should educate us. High school— college——

"Miss Mifflin got to this climax when I was thirteen or fourteen and when Dad's accumulated few thousand dollars had made him feel more secure. He had become more reasonable and pliable and gentle. He had also learned some English by this time. So in very vigorous language full of mispronounced cuss-words he declared that he would educate us so we would be 'smatt like sonafhitch.' He didn't know what 'sonafhitch' meant; he used it for emphasis.

"She influenced Dad in other respects. When union organizers first came to Dexter the roused feeling in town affected relationships even among school children. Some of us were 'union,' some 'anti-union.' Dad did not want to join because the bosses, whom he respected highly and regarded with gratitude, were of course anti-union. Besides, he did not like the idea of paying dues, did not believe the union would raise his wages, and did not mind his long hours. He was greatly interested in his job—the water in the pits was a continual challenge to him and he believed himself to be a better pumper than the man on the day shift. He was a peasant individualist. And since his work, unlike the miners', was steady, he felt no need of the union.

"Then some ugly incidents occurred. One man was beaten up; another's windows were stoned. This outraged Miss Mifflin and she convinced Dad he should sign up. Without explaining how she knew, she said he would not be discharged for joining the union.

"I forgot to mention that after we moved to the little house Dad all but broke with the Lemko or Carpathian group in Dexter. He had belonged to the Uniate parish in town; now he ceased going to church. I think he resented the lack of Christian feeling, after Mother's death, in the women of the parish. Not even his cousin's wife or his mother-in-law had volunteered to help him with his children. Perhaps they wanted to drive him into remarriage. I suspect my grandmother wanted him to marry the inept aunt who tried to keep house for us. When she saw he had no such intention she probably set the others against him. It was all pretty primitive. But whatever the reason for their neglect he wanted to get even—somehow. For two or three years he talked to almost no one except the men in the mine, the storekeepers, and Miss Mifflin. Before we knew Miss Mifflin he insisted that Annie and I have no avoidable contact with people and we largely obeyed him.

He would not let us go to church either. The two youngest children were indoors all the time.

"Miss Mifflin gradually broke down these regulations. We began to make friends and go to church. I joined a gang of boys of several different backgrounds: Lemko, Russian, Ukrainian, Italian, Slovak, and Montenegrin. We chewed tobacco, smoked black stogies, flung dead cats on the porches of people we didn't like, called one another Hunkies and Wops in fun, but fought it out with any outsider who called us names.

"I never ran our gang or anything like that; I merely followed along. The leader I remember best was Pete Markovich, a Montenegrin miner's son. He was a tall, rawboned fellow of seventeen, fair and honest, the strongest in the gang. Once he knocked down a boy named Roger Thomas—a brother of the girl who had offered me the apple in the first grade—for contemptuously referring to one of the gang as a Catholic. (Pete himself was *pravoslavni*, of the Serbian Orthodox Church.) And he kicked all over the lot two boys who had tied a can to a dog's tail. Pete was firm too in his disapproval of all sexual experimentation at our age. He told us of a talking-to which his uncle had given him on the subject. . . .

"Esther Thomas was always a term or two ahead of me in school, but for years I saw her every few days. I acted as though she were just another girl, but now and then I suffered acutely in secret. Talk about inferiority! She was 'American' way back; my father was a foreigner. Her name was Thomas; mine Sobuchanowsky. She lived in a big white house over in the 'nice' part of town, her father was rich, she wore beautiful clothes and she was very good-looking, while I was a skinny little guy. She went to Vassar; I went to Monongahela College in Blacksburg. After high school they moved away and I never saw her again; her father became manager of a mill in Pittsburgh.

Several years later I saw in some paper that she and her mother were traveling in Europe.

"After Miss Mifflin, who thought we needed some contact with religion, broke down Dad's opposition the question arose: which brand? The Uniates were disbanded; they had gradually lost out to the three 'real' Catholic churches—Irish, Slovak, Polish—and the Russian Orthodox church. Dad dithered over which we should choose. He burst forth to Miss Mifflin with old prejudices and grievances: they were equally bad. Miss Mifflin suggested the Irish church. Father exploded. He did not like the Irish because the Irish hated the 'foreigners.'

"There was an *impasse*. Neither Annie nor I at twelve or thirteen knew which faith we wanted to embrace, while Mike and Joe were too young to be asked. Miss Mifflin, not herself a churchgoing woman, finally suggested we try them all. Dad thought this sheer wisdom.

"So we started with the Russian church. It was a strange and colorful building, I imagine much like a village church in Russia; but none of us liked it enough to stick to it. There was a lot of singing by the bearded priest that sounded nice at first, but we couldn't understand it and it ceased to impress us.

"One Sunday we went to the Slovak Catholic church. Then we tried the Polish church. We did not feel particularly at home in either. Joe, who was not yet ten, came along only because Annie and I dragged him. He was miserable and sullen.

"This went on for about a year. Then Annie and I decided to see what a Protestant church was like. The congregation were regular 'Americans,' all well dressed; the children gaped at us. We went only once.

"Sometime later Pete Markovich asked me one day which church we went to. I told him none lately and he took us to the Serbian *pravoslavna*, in a neighboring town.

It resembled the Russian church; we liked it a while, then gave it up too.

"In short, our contact with religion was haphazard, as was our general upbringing.

"Miss Mifflin did her best, and really worked wonders in our family. But in 1918 when the flu epidemic hit Dexter she came down with it and died.

"Half the people in town were ill including all of us except Dad (nothing ever touched him), and we did not hear about Miss Mifflin till after she had been sent away in a coffin; then all four of us children broke out crying, while Dad left the house and probably vented his grief behind the culm dump again.

"We were still too young to think of trying to find out about Miss Mifflin—who she was, where she had come from, where she was buried, how she had known Dad's job was safe when she told him to join the union. Strangely enough, we did not even know where she had lived in Dexter. We had taken her as she was, the way she had taken us.

COLLEGE, A NEW NAME, AND A JOB

"I GRADUATED from high school with seconds honors, while Annie was fourth on the list of about two hundred; and Mike and Joe, coming up behind us, both had above-average records.

"Our graduation was a great personal triumph for Dad. In those days few 'foreign' youngsters finished high school, and here were two of his children at one throw. He was in a fidget of excitement although he grieved that Meez Meef was not present. He wore a new suit, new shoes, a new hat; and we had new outfits too. Dad let us buy what we wished. He wanted us to be like the rest of the youngsters. 'Like odder Americans, you betchya!' He now had around seven thousand dollars, all of it destined for our education.

"Dad insisted on putting all of us through college. I went, as I say, to Monongahela. Annie stayed home a year after high school and kept house. She was so conscience-stricken about going away to live 'like a lady' while Father slaved in the mine that for a time she thought she couldn't do it. Dad got mad, reminding her of his promise to Meez Meef. One of the engineers at the mine had told him a student could do very well at college on four hundred dollars a year; so this was the annual sum he had allocated for each of us. He would not hear of our working our way through. He wanted us to have everything and every advantage others had. In short, Dad *was* 'funny.' It bothered my conscience too to take his hard-earned money; but I was more philosophical about it. I argued that putting us through college was less of a sacrifice for Dad than a self-realization. If Annie refused she would deny him some-

173

thing that probably was his due. So the following year she went to the University of West Virginia at Morgantown.

"Mike and Joe went to Pitt.

"From here on our stories diverge. I shall try to restrict myself largely to my own; much of it I can cover in a hurry.

"I liked Monongahela College, and worked hard and became a good student. I made friends readily. I majored in history; literature and English interested me. In my junior year I was editor of the literary magazine and later was elected to Phi Beta Kappa. Aside from a few slightly unpleasant experiences, there was no prejudice against me because I was 'foreign.'

"In my senior year I decided I wanted to teach English, so I went to the University of Illinois and in '29 got a Master's degree.

"That summer I did everything possible to find a college teaching position. I failed. I went back to Monongahela College for some special courses in pedagogy.

"One day Professor Clark, who was a friend of mine, asked me if I had ever thought of changing my name. He said if I didn't I might have a tough time getting into education. He thought my name might have affected my chances at college teaching. Not that colleges had any hard rule against 'foreign' names. 'Sobuchanowsky' might be perfectly all right for a professor of physics or mathematics or foreign languages; for a teacher of English it didn't sound very well.

"This bothered me. I resented his suggestion a little. But he was right. There was no place for me anywhere in western Pennsylvania, not even in my home town. Many of my applications were not so much as acknowledged. A few superintendents, especially those near Pittsburgh, informed me that nobody named Sobuchanowsky could teach English or anything else in any of their schools.

"The following fall Dr. Clark accepted an important

position in the Cleveland school system and asked me if I would care to teach in a high school there.

"I said I would of course.

"He said he needed history teachers. Then he wrote my name on a pad, looked at it a minute and said: 'Cleveland has a reputation for tolerance and liberalism; considerably over half the town is foreign-born or of immigrant parentage. But, John—' He hesitated, looking at me, then tried another tack. 'I have mentioned this before. Now I want you in Cleveland, you'll make a good history teacher. You will not be the only one with a foreign name. I have gone through the list and there are names like Gorelik, De Mario, Sedlar, and Kovach. But none that I have seen comes up to Sobuchanowsky. It will be easier for you all along the line if you will drop it and take a name like Weaver or Hays or something. Please don't misunderstand me ——'

"I interrupted him saying I understood perfectly and appreciated his interest. I said I knew he was right, but Sobuchanowsky was my name. I was twenty-seven and somewhat accustomed to it. I told him about my father: how much he had done for me, how grateful I was to him, how I honored him—I hardly knew what I was trying to say. I was upset.

"Dr. Clark asked me my father's first name.

" 'Nikolai or Nicholas,' I said. 'Everybody calls him Nick.'

" 'Well,' he said, 'why not take some form of your father's first name for your surname—Nicholas or Nichols?'

"I asked him for two or three days to think it over.

"I went to Pittsburgh to talk with my brothers; I thought they should have a say in the matter. It might be awkward for three brothers to have different surnames.

"Mike was immediately in favor of 'Nichols.' He had been job-hunting and was sure he had been turned down because of 'Sobuchanowsky.' Joe, a reporter on the student daily at Pitt, a Communist and a self-willed young man, was of a different mind. His name was Sobuchanowsky because it was his old man's and whoever didn't like it could go to hell. If we discarded it we could go to hell too—and he walked out on us.

"Mike and I changed our names legally in a Pittsburgh court. We didn't think Dad would mind, but we felt a little guilty and decided not to tell him. A week later Mike had a job with United States Steel, where he had been rejected six weeks before, and I went to Cleveland.

"Annie approved. She had recently solved her own name problem by getting married to a man named Edward Gates.

MR. AND MRS. NICHOLS, AMERICANS

"Shortly after coming to Cleveland I met a girl named Mary Land. We did not pry into each other's past lives. She knew I came from Pennsylvania where my father was a miner; I knew she had been born on a farm in Michigan and that her parents were dead. That was all—enough.

"But when we began to see a lot of each other I thought I should tell her about my name. I still was not quite used to being Nichols. Off and on I came close to signing or introducing myself as Sobuchanowsky.

"It was difficult to open the subject. When I finally told her, I was surprised to see her go through a rapid series of moods. At first she listened to me wide-eyed; then she laughed; and finally she cried out almost frantically: 'What difference does it make! You're Nichols now! We're both Americans! It makes no difference where our parents came from.'

"She burst into tears and after a while she told me her name had been Schwabenland. Her parents were German immigrants who had had a miserable time of it during the World War. They moved to Detroit and shortened their name. Her mother died; then, a few years later, her father. He left her two thousand dollars and she had gone to Oberlin and the University of Michigan. Now at twenty-six she was secretary to a business executive in Cleveland.

"Her story, which she told abruptly, moved me terribly. I proposed to her then and there. We were married a few days later.

"When we moved into our apartment Mary typed MR. & MRS. NICHOLS on a card for our mailbox downstairs. 'Now, John,' she said firmly, 'we are Mr. and Mrs. Nichols

and that's all there is to it. We are Americans regardless
and no matter what! This is a new chapter, and what came
before is torn out of the book.'

"I nodded although what Mary said and the way she
said it disturbed me. There was such finality to her words.

"She went down to put the card in the mailbox.

"By the time she returned I had thought things over
and decided she was right. I admired her definiteness, her
ability to be what she wanted to be. She was an American
by saying she was an American—'regardless and no matter
what.' We *were* Mr. and Mrs. Nichols—'and that's all there
is to it'!

"Of course I realized that behind it all were sensitive
scars. 'Torn out of the book' meant she did not want to
talk about our origin or background ever again. But that
was all right with me. We were very much in love. We
considered ourselves very fortunate. While everybody was
beginning to worry about the depression, we both had
jobs and were earning good salaries. We read books and
went to the theater. I learned to play bridge and like
anagrams. Mary had a number of friends who took me in,
and we enjoyed some pleasant social intercourse with a
crowd of teachers I knew.

"Not that I was entirely at ease in the 'torn out of the
book' arrangement. But I was pretty sure Mary was, and
I was anxious she should remain so. When Annie and her
husband came to see us on their way to California, I
dropped a hint to them. Annie was very glad to be Mrs.
Gates, and seemed to understand my wife's desire to keep
our background under cover. She and Mary chatted about
practical things: furniture, curtains, what Annie and
Edward planned to do in California. There was no mention of Mary's parents or of Dad. If our names had always
been Gates, Land and Nichols, the conversation might have

been pretty much the same in content. But the way we talked might have been different. We were stiff, nervous and dull. There was no spontaneity or laughter. I had but recently changed my name; it would have been natural to discuss it. I wondered if Gates was my brother-in-law's real name. The material for real talk was in the room as Mary served tea, but we sat on it and it sat on us.

"It was the same when Mike came to see us. Annie had written him and he knew that Mary and I wanted to be 'just Americans.'

"But Joe had no use for any of us. He had told Mike, whom he could not entirely avoid, that the less he saw of us the better he liked it. By changing our name we had 'compromised'—and he was a Communist. We were bent on getting along no matter how. Get-alongers, he called us. To Joe, prejudice against 'foreigners' and their names was all tied up with the capitalist system. To discriminate against 'foreign' names was one way of keeping down the people who went by them. Not that he had any special affection for 'Sobuchanowsky' and he regarded Dad as a low-grade proletarian; but he did not propose to make any concession to capitalism!

"Joe's extreme attitude annoyed me. But I had moments when I could not help but respect something in him. He had spirit. Mike and I *were* 'get-alongers.' Then I thought that to get along, to compromise, was the thing to do. He was just a kid; he would get over his nonsense ——

"Meanwhile, back in Dexter Dad went on pretty much in his old way. He lived alone now in the little house. And Joe spent his summers there. He aspired to be a writer and was studying Dexter as a coal town in the grip of the depression. He was going to write a book about it. He never did. But as I later discovered, he once published a poem in the *New Masses*. . . .

"Depression or no depression, water had to be pumped out of the mine; so Dad was all right. With the years he became more sociable and took to mingling again with the Lemkoes and to drinking, smoking and playing the slot-machines. The fact that all four of his children were college graduates was a great feather in his cap. We were 'like odder Americans, smatt like sonafhitch.' We lived all over America, or so it seemed to Dad. Mike had a good job in a 'beeg offits' in Pittsburgh, which was farther than Dad would dream of venturing from Dexter. Annie was in California, married. I was married too and taught school like Meez Meef; but Cleveland was also a good distance away. He did not seem to miss seeing us. He knew that eventually even Joe would cease coming home for his vacations. That was all right with him: we were Americans.

"He met his son-in-law only once. I think that Annie, whom university education had changed somewhat, had become—not exactly ashamed of Dad but uncomfortable about him. She is proud of her go-getting husband and his string of gas stations around Los Angeles.

"Dad has never yet met my wife. Shut within her 'torn out of the book' attitude, Mary does not want to meet him. He does not exist. The question has come up in my mind hundreds of times, but never verbally between us.

"On his side Dad seems perfectly satisfied to know I am married to an 'American' woman. He always asks how she is but that is all. She is an 'American' and she lives in distant Cleveland and has a 'jopp in a beeg offits'— ample explanation to his peasant mind why she has not come to see him. There is this too: he is punctual in going to work, but I have a feeling that time is not important to him. He is not conscious of the years as they slip by. He will meet my wife eventually; if not now, next time. It does not matter when. He is in no hurry. Which may contradict some of the other things I have mentioned:

for one, the fury with which he has worked to earn money. But as I say he is a complicated human being: a peasant.

"I didn't see Dad for over a year after I was married. Dexter is only a few hours' drive from Cleveland, but somewhat I couldn't bring myself to go.

"Then one night while Mary was in New York on business for her boss I drove down on an impulse. I had expected Dad to be in the mine. But there was a light in the house. Suddenly I felt almost afraid to go in. After a while I made myself rap on the door. I heard someone moving around upstairs; then Joe leaned out of the window and yelled down. Who was I and what did I want?

"I said, 'Hello, Joe—this is John.'

"Joe only grunted. After a while he came down to let me in. He looked at me with a sneer for what seemed at least a minute, then told me to make myself at home. 'Why not?' he said. 'After all, Mr. Nichols, you *are* one of the Sobuchanowskys too.'

"I didn't want to start an argument. There was nothing to say anyhow.

"Joe went back upstairs.

"I lay down on Dad's unmade bed and couldn't go to sleep. The bed smelled. I went over the whole story of our family. There was neither rhyme nor reason to it.

"In the morning when Dad got home I had made breakfast on the old stove. He was glad to see me, but matter-of-fact as though I had been gone only a couple of days and had returned just when he expected me to. He asked me only the simplest questions: When did I come? When did I buy my car? How long would I stay? How was my health? Was my woman well, too? I still had my 'jopp'?

"He was dirty, bent and tired, and I made him go to bed.

"In the afternoon I walked with him up and down Main Street. He went about his shopping. He stepped into a near-beer place and I followed him in. He put two nickels in a slot-machine, lost both, and gave a twisted smile, shaking his head. He was a caricature of a man, terribly skinny, weighing less than a hundred pounds now but apparently in good health, so stooped he gave the weird impression of being a question mark. His abnormally long and thin arms swung beside him far and wide; his hands reached almost to his knees. My feelings were all mixed up. I was ashamed of him, and at the same time I wanted to kneel down at his feet in public. I suppose this is the Slav in me. . . . Anyway, as Dad and I walked on Main Street and met people I had known in high school I introduced him as my father, and I wanted to add: 'to whom I owe everything.'

"Telling you all this makes me wince, but there is also a strange pleasure, something akin to what the medieval flagellants must have felt. I said I would tell you the truth, and I am probing as deeply as I can, which makes me feel noble. 'Noble' is not quite the word but you know what I mean. I feel also like a low-life, just as I felt with Dad on Main Street ——

"Dad cooked supper that afternoon, as he had when we were children. Joe had disappeared, and Dad and I ate alone. The way he served the food, the way he ate, would have disgusted our Cleveland friends, and the food was crude. But I ate with a curious enjoyment. Dad talked a little, in his native language peppered with ill-pronounced English words and phrases, and I found a satisfaction in being able to understand him. He bustled about the kitchen, he ran upstairs; there was still much of the old frantic, furtive manner about him. He shrugged his shoulders about 'Tchoe.'

"He made thick boloney sandwiches exactly as he had made them when I was a boy; but I noticed he put an apple in his lunch-pail. I had told him I was returning to

Cleveland that evening, so he insisted on making some sandwiches for me—I was going on a far journey.

"He washed the dishes. I dried them.

"Promptly at quarter to six we shook hands and he left for his night's work.

"I drove off. But after a while I couldn't see for the tears in my eyes. I parked somewhere and cried like an idiot. Instead of driving to Cleveland that evening, I stopped at a tourist house. I tried to get myself into a common-sense frame of mind. I told myself that of course I loved Dad, but he was impossible for Mary and our Cleveland crowd.

"Mary was right: so far as our life was concerned it *was* best for him, and my old name, to stay 'torn out of the book.' But I made up my mind to see Dad once a year at least. I would drive down when Mary went away somewhere so I would not have to explain.

"But Mary's attitude bothered me more and more. I resented her ability to maintain it. She had no qualms, no moments of imagining—so far as I could see, anyhow.

"I resented, too, the effect of her attitude on our relationship as man and wife, and simply as people; but she did not seem to realize what was happening. Sometimes we came very close to the past—to her childhood experiences and my father and all the rest—but we never discussed it. She always neatly avoided the subject. In company when talk arose about someone of foreign parentage, she would make an irrelevant remark steering the conversation into other channels. Of course on such occasions I never said anything pertinent either, but I couldn't help wondering if Mary's matter-of-fact manner wasn't just surface. Now and then she was a little tense and abrupt. Maybe beneath it she was bothered too. I wondered if it didn't require tremendous effort, which kept her from being much more vital and spontaneous. It affected me, too. Maybe I wasn't what I could be. Was I blaming Mary? Wasn't it my fault as much as hers? But I didn't follow this line of thought through. Perhaps I couldn't. What stood out most was this: Mary and I were not open with each other—a serious matter in any close relationship, particularly marriage.

"The psychological delver in me (a Slavic trait too, perhaps) wondered about all this. I asked myself if Mary's German blood explained her definiteness, and if my introspection and vacillation were Slavic. I didn't know; I couldn't decide.

"Finally, lying awake in that tourist house, I dismissed all these complicated speculations. I told myself there were more important things in life than my confusion about that poor man in Dexter. I was in love with Mary; we were to have a baby in September. My future was with her and the child. We had certain American standards and all this stewing of mine was nonsense. I was soft, wishy-washy. I must be definite, clear, hard with myself. Like Mary. She had sense. Life was raveled enough without brooding in a vicious circle.

"In the morning as a kind of symbolic gesture of my determination to go on just as Mary and I had been doing, I flung out of the car the sandwiches Dad had put in a brown paper bag for me. The next second I wanted to run my car over the bank. But then I snapped back into my 'sensible' attitude.

"This was nearly seven years ago. I have been to Dexter every summer since and twice at Easter too. Sometimes I stay two or three days, walking up and down Main Street with Dad in the afternoon.

"Betweenwhiles I have—with periodic lapses—maintained the hard, the 'sensible' attitude to which Mary and I agreed the day we moved into our apartment. We have been married eight years, and I still love my wife—if I am not required to define love. I am certainly very fond of her; I admire her. Barbara is an adorable child—six and a half, a vivid, healthy and clear personality. If I should say that I am probably happier than most husbands and fathers it would be a good guess.

"This is my ninth year in the same school in Cleveland. I like teaching, and I am considered good at it. And if I should say that I am happy in my work it would also be approximately correct.

"Between us Mary and I make nearly five hundred a month. We have a dependable woman who takes care of Barbara and the household. We live on a budget and save about half our income. Mary's boss tips her off and she has been playing the market. She lost a little in the 1937 'recession' but we are still way ahead. Eventually we plan to have a home of our own with a lawn and trees around it. We each have a car. We go out, or people call on us about once a week. In short we are typically middle-class.

"Barbara—Mary and I love her terribly, although we try to be intelligent about it. She is the most important thing we have in common and it is a lot—enough. We have hopes and plans for her. She will go to college of course: Vassar or Smith. With some luck, she will be a fine woman. I am sure of it. She is lovely now.

"Occasionally there is a little rivalry between Mary and me for her affection. It's all rather silly. But I think it adds to the tension between us. Barbara loves us both, and evenings when we are alone at home the three of us often have delightful times together before she goes to bed. Our living-room sometimes presents a 'typical American' scene —the sort of picture you see in furniture and rug advertisements.

"But ——

"In a way I have never been sorry I changed my name. Bill Clark was right; it was the practical thing to do. It is very convenient to be Nichols instead of Sobuchanowsky— but ——

"IT IS A STRANGE THING—TO BE AN AMERICAN ——"

"But every once in a while I get a terrific wrench inside me—an emotional wrench which is so intense, so close that it is almost physical. It is as though someone clutched the ends of certain vital strings within me and gave them a sudden yank. And every time this happens I find myself thinking of my father, and also that I am not really John S. Nichols, a teacher, a matter-of-fact middle-class American, but only God knows that—a fool, a low-life, a man in a trap.

"The wrench is apt to occur anywhere any time—in bed, where it jerks me awake; as I stop for a red light in the car; at home when I am teaching Barbara to read or we are looking at a picture book; in class as some pupil recites or as I assign homework. It happens frequently, but it hits me especially badly four or five times a year and makes me abrupt, impatient. I have the impulse to smash something, anything; it is hard to control my temper— even toward Barbara. As for Mary, when I get in that state I try to avoid her till I dig myself out. I usually succeed in a few hours but sometimes it takes a day or two.

"What is this—what are these periodic wrenches? Any connection between them and my name? A little, yes, but perhaps not in any real way. Would I get them if I were still Sobuchanowsky? Possibly. Would they be any different. I don't know. But actually I am beginning to see that it is not my past but all this concealment that fills me with fear. I see now that I am continually acting out of fear. I am not free; I don't act freely. I say I am a man in a trap; it is no exaggeration. Is Mary the trap? I say I love her. Do I? I certainly hate her 'torn out of the book' idea. She refuses to talk of our past. She won't let me talk. I can't mention my father to her. Or to Barbara, for that matter. I can't ask her what her trouble is. I am afraid of her. I blame her. Do I hate her? I don't know. . . . These ideas and questions have sprung up in my head as I talk. I have never let myself think this way before.

"Until this minute I thought these spasms were chiefly mixed up with my father. I think of him often between-times, only not so sharply. I don't get upset. I am philosophical about him and the rest of the family. Or I think I am. Then all of a sudden I am sunk again.

"If it happens at home I say that I have a headache and want to go out alone. I take a long walk or a drive. Sometimes I park my car somewhere and argue myself back into the 'sensible' frame of mind. Or I go to a movie or a lecture. If I am driving home, I phone the house that I will be late. If it occurs at night, I can't stay in the same room with Mary and listen to her breathing. Maybe I do hate her at such moments. But if I do, I don't at the same time; for when one of these fits seizes me, my regular 'sensible' self stays and has at least a partial sway over my feelings and behavior. I always *know* Mary is a fine person and that I cannot really have anything against her—although come to think of it, this is not quite true. I think she is a fine person, but I force myself to think so.

"She never hears me get up. I go in the living-room, where I turn on the light over my reading-chair and open a book as an excuse if she should chance to wake and come in to see what I am doing up so late. Sometimes I quietly leave the apartment and walk for a few hours, and return feeling better—convinced once more that Mary is right, that she is wise. Anyhow I have adhered to her idea for so long there is now no way out of it.

"I know that many old-stock Americans on their way

up in the world hide what they consider their lowly beginnings. But their problem is comparatively simple. In
a case like mine there are all sorts of other complications.

"Take what happened today in a class. I asked a question
in American history, and a student used the phrase 'our
forefathers.' He was quoting from the chapter in our text-
book on the founding of the Republic. The boy's name is
Italian, and if I am not mistaken his parents are not even
United States citizens. This struck me as ludicrous and I
thought to myself, '*Our* forefathers—nonsense!'

"The bell rang and I left the class. Then I found myself
suddenly writhing inside. It was absurd that *I* should be
teaching American history, certainly from the kind of book
which I was required to use—*I*, whose 'real' name was
Sobuchanowsky and whose father was a 'funny'-looking
foreigner, an alien, a Lemko—one of a tribe that hardly
anybody in the United States ever heard of.

"I was walking down a corridor carrying a couple of
books, and I wanted to smash them through a window.

"It was my last class today. I got out of the building and
drove into the country, then went for a walk. I struggled
through the usual process of getting myself back into a
'sensible' frame of mind. I called myself a fool, a hysteric.
Mary was right; we *were* Americans . . . and so on and
so on. At the same time, I recognized a feeling which had
come to me before during one of these periods, but never
so clearly and sharply, that my life—our life—had a dim,
muffled quality.

"Returning to my car, I looked at the morning paper
which I hadn't yet read, and I happened to see that you
were lecturing on 'Plymouth Rock and Ellis Island.'

"I drove downtown, had an early supper and went to a
movie. During the show, the phrase 'Plymouth Rock and
Ellis Island' kept popping up into my mind ——

A POSTCARD FROM JOE SOBUCHANOWSKY

"There are other things in my story which make it rather different from that of the average old-stock American who is hiding something connected with his origin or youth. For one thing, there is the rest of the family.

"Annie and I haven't seen each other since she left for California. Her letters, like mine, touch only superficial things. Whether or not this covers her life I don't know; I doubt if it does. She sends us and Dad boxes of dried California fruit, which impresses him very much—it is sheer luxury, a new proof every time that Annie is 'like an American.'

"Mike I see less and less often as the years go on. He still works for United States Steel—in a routine job; he has probably not had a raise since '38. The last few times we met he seemed downright dull. I don't understand it; as a boy he was rather bright. Now the only thing that excites him is football. He is unmarried and lives in a hotel room. He is 'Mike Nichols' and I suppose none of his acquaintances know that his name once was Sobuchanowsky and that he has a Hunky father in Dexter. He certainly seems to have forgotten Dad. He hasn't been home for four years. Has the change of name done that to him? Or would he have been that way anyway? . . .

"Joe is a different story. After he was graduated from Pitt, Mike and I lost all trace of him. Then summer before last I found him in Dexter. When he saw me he yelled out, 'Oh hello, Mr. Nichols!' He was extremely unpleasant and seemed almost disbalanced. There were moments, though, when he called me John and talked as if he wanted to be friends. I learned he had been active in the Communist party in New York. One day he put a copy of the *New Masses* containing his poem where I could not miss seeing it. It was signed 'Joe Sobuchanowsky.' It was about Pittsburgh—steel mills, smoke and grime, workers and capitalists. There was a kind of power; there were some good lines; but I did not like it as a whole and I couldn't bring myself to comment upon it. This enraged Joe and he resumed calling me 'Mr. Nichols' and being disagreeable.

"So far as I could make out he had no plans. I did not like him but he worried me. Dad accepted him: he was an American and Americans were strange people. He gave him money and shrugged his shoulders as though to say, there he is, what can I do? I decided there was nothing I could do either.

"When I left, Joe was not home. So on an impulse I stuck a note in his room, saying good-by and telling him to let me know if I could ever be of any help. I put my address at the bottom.

"Last summer when I went to Dexter again Joe was not there. I asked Dad about him. He shrugged his shoulders and said, 'Tchoe he go 'way.'—'When?'—Dad said, 'After Noo Year he go.'

"Then last week I received a postcard from Joe. It was mailed from Tacoma, Washington, and all it said was: 'You remember me, Mr. Nichols? Your brother (ha! ha!).' This worried me. It sounded cracked. What was he doing in Tacoma? Was he sent out there by the Communist party? But what directly concerned me was that he had addressed the card 'John Sobuchanowsky Nichols.' I thought at once, 'My God, the postman saw it!'

"This postman has been delivering our mail for five or six years. In many ways he is a perfectly decent man. He considers himself a patriotic American but he is full of strong prejudices. He doesn't like 'foreigners' or Jews or

Catholics, and thinks 'niggers' should be kept in their place. He is a friend of Marcus Brown, a property owner in the section who rents only to 'Americans' and 'Christians,' and the postman I suspect keeps him informed on what is going on in the neighborhood. Not that he is a spy; probably he and Mr. Brown merely gossip.

"Since the card came I have been sure the rumor was out that I was some kind of 'foreigner.' The greetings of the garagemen have been a little different.

"Mary doesn't know anything yet, and may not ever. Maybe no issue will be made of it. But—I don't know. Only yesterday morning as I came down, the postman seemed to want to talk with me. I think he had even waited for me, but I pretended to be in a great hurry. . . . It is all very cheap and narrow. It is unfair and stupid. I have no words to say how I despise it all.

"I try not to worry about gossip, but I do. I haven't slept well this week. I keep wondering: Suppose Mary should get wind of it? What will she say? Will it open up the whole business between us? Suppose it does? Suppose it gets to our school friends? I might have to explain to them. It would be awkward at the very least. Then what? I don't know.

"I'm confused. I guess I'm rambling.

"Maybe nothing will happen, and Mary and I will go on as we began. Only if we go on this way I am afraid that, with this intellectual and emotional no-man's land between us, our relationship will get worse and worse. It is as I say quite dim and muffled already. Unnatural. Tense and, at the same time, weary. Shot through with a kind of nervousness partly from me but chiefly, I think, from Mary—from the quality most consistently apparent in her personality, manner and actions—although I am beginning to wonder if it may be my fault as much as hers. Or more than hers.

"I shouldn't be telling you all this . . . but I have got

started and I may as well complete the picture if I can.
. . . Mary is never at ease when she is alone with me. It
is as though she suspects perhaps unconsciously that I
have something on my mind, not necessarily at the moment but in general, and she is afraid I will bring it up.
She talks a great deal—obviously to keep me from saying
anything. It is a kind of censorship.

"She has developed a number of dodges and escapes. In
her brief case when she comes home evenings there is
usually some work from the office, so that if it looks as
though our conversation might get dangerous she can suddenly say, 'Oh dear, do you mind? I have some letters to
type; Mr. Sumners wants them the first thing in the morning.' Or she abruptly takes a notion to telephone somebody about nothing at all. Or she turns on the radio. Or
she has a book she is terribly enthusiastic about; she has
to finish it tonight so she can return it to the lending
library tomorrow. Or she suddenly pleads weariness—
although two minutes before she has treated me to a lively
monologue.

"This sort of thing has become pretty clear to me the
last year or so. God knows what actually goes on inside
of her. I can only speculate about the symptoms.

"As a result I am pretty self-conscious with her. I tell
myself she is very complex, but this is not particularly
comforting. I am not a psychiatrist; I am her husband. Of
course there may be something wrong with me. No doubt
there is. I have let myself get into a trap. Now . . . now
I am not man enough to get out of it.

"Naturally, Barbara feels something is wrong between
her mother and me. You can't fool children about these
things—although of course she wouldn't put it that way.
Not yet.

"Now things are controlled, held down. Suppose they
should erupt into open daylight where we would have to
look at them together. That would be drastic. I have no

idea how Mary would act. It might conceivably be an immense relief to her if the whole 'torn out of the book' structure suddenly collapsed. But it might possibly break up our marriage. I am afraid. I don't really know Mary.

"And Barbara? I don't know, I don't know. She is terribly precious to me. I can't risk losing her.

"I wish Bill Clark were still here. We were friends. He was the only man in Cleveland who knew that Nichols was not my original name. I could have gone to him and talked, and this whole mix-up might not have developed so far. But he left Cleveland after less than a year to become president of a teachers' college out West. I haven't seen him since although we keep up. But I can't bring myself to write him about my difficulty. It would make an awfully long letter. It might sound as though I blamed him for inducing me to change my name. I might not make it clear enough that that is merely the surface summation of the whole business. . . .

"Should my 'foreign' name burst into the open, it is apt to affect my professional standing. My teaching might become less effective. Even pupils of Slavic parentage might lose their respect for me. How can a man named Sobuchanowsky speak of 'our Founding Fathers'? Even as John Nichols I have a hard time giving *myself* a sense of reality in the classroom. That a youngster named Quattrociocchi should talk about 'our forefathers' struck me as ludicrous; if it gets out that I am 'really' Sobuchanowsky, I may well sound ludicrous to the students.

"My whole teaching relationship is rather unreal—and quite in keeping with my personal mess. Our school is considered one of the best in the city. But I wonder. A high percentage of our pupils are sons and daughters of immigrants: Italian, Polish, Slovenian, Jewish, Czech, Hungarian. Yet the textbooks pay next to no attention to this fact. And we teachers proceed routine fashion on the assumption that youngsters named Podreznik, Ruspini, Valentincich, Zlamal, Ruminskinski, Utz, Evankovitz and Bosnyak have the same background as those named Wells and Price. But there is a terrible contradiction. While our formal presentation of material presupposes the same background, the rest of our behavior makes a distinction between our 'American' pupils and the children with 'foreign' names.

"There is no direct, intentional discrimination against these students. Most of us try to pronounce their names correctly. Nonetheless, I suspect our unconscious attitude helps to put some of them on the spot. They get miserable without knowing why, or hell-bent on being one-hundred-percenters although they have no idea what it means to be an American. Neither have we. All they are after is to be different from their 'foreign' parents, with their 'funny' ways brought over from the old country.

"Few teachers whom I know at all well are aware of this. Fewer care about it. I care but do nothing, and I despise myself for it. My personal situation inhibits me from speaking out in faculty meetings or doing anything in the open which may be at variance with the work, procedure and aims of the other teachers, the principal, the school and the system. I am not a leader; I am afraid to stand out. I do do a little on the quiet—almost subversively.

"Every term I single out some youngster named Lupishinsky or Podpratnikar who seems to be troubled by something inside and around him that he cannot understand, and I try to help him. I try to make him feel that it is perfectly all right to have foreign-born parents, that he is no less American, no less valuable as a person. I tell him that in a sense we are all foreigners here except perhaps the Indians. Sometimes I look up the youngster's parents. In this way I do a little good and I feel some

satisfaction. I am doing what Miss Mifflin did, only not
as well. I haven't her independence of character, her complete unself-consciousness. I am not—I am not free. At
times I feel like a sneak and a fake. I never have the guts to
tell a student that I too am the son of an immigrant. Nor
can I bring myself to tell his parents that my father also
is a foreigner.

"As to Dad, I am sure he is outside all this. There he is
in Dexter pretty much as he always was. He works, eats,
sleeps, saves his money. In his close, narrow way he is
content with himself. He thinks he has made the grade in
America. And *he* has ——"

MY TRAIN SCHEDULE INTERRUPTS
MR. NICHOLS

I HAD told Mr. Nichols to take all the time he needed to tell me his story, but now it was late and I was obliged to interrupt him. I was on a scheduled tour and had to catch a train.

He apologized, said he was through anyhow and thanked me for listening. "I have long wanted to spill myself out to somebody. I hope you don't mind my picking on you. It just happened that way. It had to be a stranger."

I assured him that his story interested me very much, and added that I should like to keep in touch with him and eventually see him again.

"I just wanted to spill myself out," he repeated, taking his hat and coat. He was very pale. His hands trembled from near-exhaustion. "I am not asking advice. I guess no one can help me."

I said he was probably right and saw him to the elevator.

"Perhaps things will go from bad to worse," he went on. "Or they will work themselves out. Somehow. When all is said and done it's Barbara I am really concerned about. . . . Good-by! Thank you again. Good night!"

About two weeks later I wrote John Nichols in care of his school. I did not want to lose touch with him. Would he be so good as to write me a letter every once in a while? I was much interested in him, and concerned.

There was no answer.

I wrote again. Still no answer. Perhaps he was sorry he had talked to me. Perhaps this was his way of asking me to forget the whole business.

But I came upon things every now and then that reminded me of the Nicholses. Late in 1940 when I chanced to be in Cleveland I looked him up in the telephone book; the number had been disconnected. I called the high school and was told Mr. Nichols had resigned the previous spring.

I decided it would be best to forget all about it.

Still I could not help speculating. Had their predicament come to a crisis? How? With what result? Had John and Mary broken up? Had she gone off with Barbara? Or had they left Cleveland to live on a different basis elsewhere?

Then I suddenly received a long letter from John S. Nichols. The return address on the envelope was that of the western teachers' college headed by Dr. William Clark.

THE GLOW AND PAIN OF TRUTH

March 10, 1941.

"I MUST apologize . . . your two letters . . . two years ago. I hope you will forgive me. I knew right along that I would write to you eventually. . . .

"Perhaps you remember what I told you in your hotel room. Much water has since gone over the dam.

"Well, opening myself up to you that evening did curious things to me. I nearly fainted going down in the elevator. Then I sat in a big leather chair in the lobby and remained there for I don't know how long. As you checked out you passed me, but you did not see me because I hid my face and you were in a hurry.

"Why did I cover up my face? I suppose I was ashamed of myself—although this puts it too simply. You, my most recent acquaintance, were the only person in the world who knew the inside of my story, who knew me. This was disturbing. You had listened sympathetically enough; you understood what I was saying. But I really was nothing to you. And so you could be objective; you could see me better than I saw myself. This was what bothered me.

"When you stepped out of the elevator and went by me, I imagined—I was sure—you had me in mind. *What were you thinking?* That I was no good, vague, wishy-washy? That I was mostly a 'get-alonger'? Perhaps you thought I could not be a good teacher. That my admiration for Miss Mifflin was a little put on, more mental than felt. I honored her with but a token emulation, only because I thought I should. You might have thought me cold, unfeeling, suffused with self-pity, more concerned about *how* I felt about Dad than about Dad himself. That what I needed was a kick in the pants. That if I let things slide my wife and I were bound to crack up.

"What were you thinking of her? That she needed a kick of some kind too? Or that I blamed her for what was chiefly my fault? Maybe you believed I hated her because I was not man enough to cope with her 'torn out of the book' decision. The conflict, with Mary's nervousness and my symptomatic 'wrenches,' raged and sizzled about me, and I made no effort to deal with reality. I had no guts—just wanted to get along. I was afraid—my job, my marriage. I felt deeply only about Barbara.

"What *were* you thinking as you drove in the cab to the station? That I was blindly determined to have a different life in Cleveland than I had had as a boy in Dexter? Perhaps I was no different than the 'foreign' youngsters in my school. Their fathers too were born abroad. Did you think *I* was hell-bent on being an American? A poor devil, victim of my particular circumstances? Maybe I did feel badly about my father and was disturbed about Joe. Maybe Mike's mediocrity did shock me. I was really concerned about the tension slowly wrecking my marriage. I was caught in a hierarchy of values which were not fundamentally mine, and so many things were against me that I could not examine them and did not know what to do or where to turn. I was a little frantic. I went off by myself when I was hurt—no, that was Dad. 'Frantic, furtive.' Could it be that I was like Dad? I saved money too. I was lonely. Things were against me as other things had been against him. The scale of values he met when he started out in America were not basically his either. We were a lot alike. Was *that* what you were thinking as you got in your Pullman?

"Were you thinking that I could not face having it out with Mary? I had my wrenches, walked, rode, went to movies and lectures, was afraid I might lose Mary because she was important to my scheme of respectability and 'getting along.' But above all—Barbara ——

"Or *what?* What were you thinking? There must be a spark of something genuine in me or I would have cut away from my past long ago without looking back at Dad and worrying about Joe. Wouldn't I have concealed forever my antecedents? Did you think: Just a neurotic? Or: He is of Slavic descent, poor guy, maybe he has a soul?

"For a moment sitting on that leather chair in the lobby I smiled at the absurdity of this last thought. Then I squirmed, regretting I had talked to you. Who were you anyhow to know so much about me? Of course you hadn't dragged the story out of me; I had barged in on you and asked you to listen, and you had—without comment. You were tired. You had listened to me as long as you could without missing your train. Now, in your berth, before going to sleep, you were thinking all sorts of things and I had no chance to reply. The next day you were lecturing in Chicago on second-generation 'difficulties'—what an understatement! You might tell about *me.* I knew you would not use my name, but the idea of your talking about me was intolerable. Somerset Maugham says that everything a writer hears or sees is inevitably his material. You might write me up! Suddenly one day I'd open a magazine or a book and there would be my story. You wouldn't call me Nichols, and you would change the place names, but ——

"I had been a damn fool! I would have given anything to erase my story from your mind.

"I seldom drink; but now I went into the bar and ordered Scotch. I had two; then gradually I stopped stewing. I realized that it was I who had been thinking and blaming it on you. I was thinking about myself as never before. Talking to you had removed a block, had released something in me. I was still exhausted; my hands shook;

they were bloodless; but somehow I felt extraordinarily fine. A glow was spreading inside me—not just the whisky. The core of this glow was a thin-drawn feeling, sharp and close to ecstasy. I had told you the truth about myself!

"This was awfully important. I had told you the truth about myself, and as a result I saw myself as I was. Not an inspiring sight—yet I experienced a deep elation. I felt free. I thought perhaps truth in itself, the seeing of it, gives joy even if the facts are painful. It freed me of fear. Talking to you, who listened impersonally, made me see things that had been held down, and gave me a new slant on myself. The new slant, I remembered, had begun to creep on me in your room. All of a sudden it had then occurred to me that although I had said I loved her I *might* hate Mary. *Did* I hate her? I still didn't know. I knew I blamed her, bitterly. Could it be that I hated myself for blaming her? Could it be that I was ashamed of Dad, that I didn't want Mary to meet him? . . .

"This was something to think about.

"I remember leaving the hotel and going for my car in the parking-lot; when I found myself in front of our apartment-house, however, I had no idea how I got there. It was past three o'clock.

"Mary stirred but did not wake. I did not turn on the light. I fell asleep at once, and slept till Barbara shook me in the morning.

"The glow lasted about a week. Nobody knew anything about it. Toward Mary I behaved as usual. Evenings at home I read a great deal; and sometimes I just looked at the page before me thinking: 'Mary and I have to have it out. Soon. How will I get at her?'

"Then I had a relapse. I felt afraid and a fool again. I was sorry I had talked to you.

"About this time came your first letter asking me to keep in touch with you. It was agony. I was sure you were

going to write about me. You would figure out some ending. I resented you intensely. What right had you to
imagine how my story would end? Who did you think you
were anyhow?

"I tried to imagine your imaginings about our future.
Then I realized I was actually engaging in speculations of
my own about what would happen to us, and presently I
began to feel better.

"But I decided not to answer your letter till I had something definite to tell you.

"Now I felt fine again. I was calm. I kept examining myself and everything around me, my past and present and
future. Suppose I had stayed Sobuchanowsky? Would my
life have been different? Mary might not have wanted to
go around with me. I would have married someone else or
not at all. Had I remained Sobuchanowsky my life would
have been different in other ways too. The name might
have been a recurrent nuisance. Perhaps I would have
seemed incongruous teaching American history. But I
would not have had this dominating, pervasive fear. . . .

"The trouble of course was not the change of name; it
was that through fear I kept the change secret. Nor was
that all. I had absolved myself from action by putting the
blame squarely on Mary. I had hated her; and I had hated
myself for hating her; and had hated her again because I
had hated myself—a vicious circle.

"Now I no longer hated her. Nor myself. I was in a
curious state. I had a persistent illogical feeling that now—
soon—everything would be all right. I loved Barbara
peacefully now, not almost desperately. And also most of
the time I felt quite confident about Mary. She went on
in her own way, half-unconsciously and perpetually on
guard against me. She recognized no change in me, although now I was very quiet. I was awfully sorry for her.
(I was smug—'saved'; now I wanted to 'save' her.) I wanted

to put my arms around her and comfort her and say, 'It's all right; everything is all right now.'

"I did nothing of the sort. I knew that however we came out of this, it would be tough on both of us. I knew I would have to be hard. I rather enjoyed the prospect in a way. There was still a left-over of my hatred and I relished the idea that she would suffer. I was in no hurry to take the first step. I did not know yet what it should be and anyway I wanted to be careful. And, too, I found a dubious satisfaction in watching Mary spinning in her trap, while I was already well on the way to freedom. A less questionable satisfaction rose from imagining that I would deliver her too. (What a strange, cruel creature man is, in a way, isn't he?) I had a secret sense of superiority—not only to Mary but to everybody—and I hugged it. It was as though I had discovered something no one else knew, a hidden private world that was infinitely better than anything anyone else had. But slowly I stopped being possessive about it and began to want to share my new world. I had tasted truth and freedom. I was a new man. And I felt good. I also felt self-conscious ——

"All this sounds complicated but it is really simplified. Those first few weeks after I saw you were marked by many more ups and downs. When I felt best, there were moments when I came close to backsliding into a wrench. I was filled with remorse over my father. I blamed Mary more than myself. And I raged against our history and environment.

"Some of the stewing was provoked by the world around me. The effect of the postman's gossip lasted for a couple of weeks—chiefly in the manner of people with whom I came more or less regularly in contact. Especially different was one of the garagemen, a K.K.K. Then the gossip died down. It did not reach Mary, perhaps because by now her defenses and insulations were so strong as to be automatic; she was unaware of much going on about her—and her lack of contact with things kept upsetting me.

"Also I could not stop thinking of Joe. Every morning as I took in the mail I thought there might be another crazy card from him. I wondered about him. What was he doing out West? Was he still a Communist?

GRANDFATHERS HAVE THEIR USES

"About a year earlier Mary had decided to send Barbara to an excellent and 'exclusive' private school. At the time I had agreed. We could afford it all right. Barbara was our only child and nothing was too good for her. Now, however, partly to oppose Mary for a change but also because the idea no longer appealed to me, I started to propagandize Barbara in favor of public school.

"The child too has a touch of my father in her; she is for spending as little as possible. And with my indirect help she came to believe that since public school was free she did not want to go to private school. Her decision, suddenly announced to us one evening, rested on these further considerations: public schools were much larger than private ones, and I taught in one of the former.

"This bewildered Mary. She told Barbara we thought it best for her to go to a private school.

"Barbara turned to me.

"I said yes, I had agreed with Mummy some time ago, but if she wished to go to public school I was in favor of it. I added that she seemed to know her own mind, and I was for following her idea through. I did not hide the fact that I was delighted with her.

"Mary stared at me: there was more to this than met the eye. She said, 'But all kinds of brats—all kinds of children go to public schools!'

"Barbara, whose stubborn persevering streak comes from her mother or from my father, or from both, asked *what* kind of children.

"Mary had no ready answer.

"So I said all kinds of children went to public school:

good, bad and indifferent, bright and dumb, small and overgrown, fat and thin, boys and girls, poor and well-to-do. But also they were all the same: just a lot of kids.

" 'What's wrong with that, Mummy?' asked Barbara.

" 'Oh they are all mixed up, Barbara,' said Mary, still uncertain where her argument was taking her, for here apparently was some kind of rebellion. 'White, black and foreign children all together. You don't want to go to a school like that, darling.'

"At this point Barbara began to amaze me as she had sometimes amazed me before. She asked, 'I am white, ain't I, Mummy?'

" 'Don't say *ain't*, darling,' said Mary. 'Say *am I not*.'

" 'Am I not, Mummy?' said Barbara. 'Am I not, Daddy?'

"I said, 'Yes, you are, Barbara.'

" 'Of course you are white,' said Mary.

" 'Am I a foreigner?'

" '*No!*' cried Mary—and in a lowered voice, 'Of course not!'

" 'Is it wrong to be black or a foreigner?' was Barbara's next question. 'Are they bad?'

"Mary was wide-eyed. 'Who gave you these ideas, Barbara?'

" 'Nobody.'

" 'Why do you ask all these questions?' There was just a trace of sharpness in Mary's voice. Her eyes darted from Barbara to me, from me to Barbara.

"I said, 'They are very interesting questions.' I knew my remark was cruel and I was sorry for Mary, but I looked at her as hard as I could. I had no explanation for Barbara's questions except that she was growing up, and that Mary's remarks carried implications that Barbara caught. But I was sure we were close to the verge of something or other.

"Mary said, 'What do you mean?'

"I repeated, 'They are very interesting questions.'

"Mary stiffened and said, 'Well then, Barbara, Daddy

will answer your questions for you. I am awfully tired and
I have a headache.' She kissed Barbara good night and said,
'Daddy will see you to bed, darling, when you get ready.'
And she left the living-room. She was pale as a sheet. When
I got to bed an hour or so later she lay still as though
asleep.

"In the morning it seemed that to Mary the incident
was just one of those things that came up every so often,
serious only because it involved Barbara. In dealing with
it she had employed her usual dodge.

"But I knew I had hit on a way to cope with her. I
would oppose her instead of agreeing. If necessary I would
be cruel; for when you act out of fear or desperation you
are cruel. I still swung between blaming her and blaming
myself for our unhappy relationship. There were times
during that spring when spasms of hate clutched me as I
refused to go out or stay home or as I told her that what
she wanted Barbara to do was not good for her. By and
large, however, I was deliberate. I was out to break
through her attitude for the sake of us all. I had to crack
the shell she had built around herself.

"More than once during the summer the shell came
close to cracking. Occasionally I was quite sharp, and once
she exclaimed, 'What's the matter with you, John?' I
said, 'What's the matter with *you?*'

"We glared at each other then let the matter drop. I
had no difficulty in glaring. I was as furious at her as I was
sorry for her.

"She oscillated between snapping back at me and acting the martyr. We went to a lot of movies, but seldom to
one we both wanted to see. We had a hard time agreeing
on whom we would ask to the house, or to whose house
we would go for bridge and chatter. It was horrid—but
also a little comical now that I look back on it.

"I took good care not to turn Barbara away from her

mother, but I also exerted all my wiles and tricks to give the frequent impression that Barbara liked me more than Mary.

"It was a relief that summer to have something outside our trouble to turn to, and I worked hard on my Ph.D. thesis.

"In mid-August I made my annual visit to Dexter. It was like all the others except that Joe wasn't home. I told Dad that Joe had sent me a postcard from Tacoma, Washington. Dad did not know where Tacoma was. He merely nodded and shrugged his shoulders. I said to myself, 'What a strange duck!' yet I was quite at ease with him—for the first time in my life. I thought, 'He is strange, but he is all right; and, by God, I don't care what anybody thinks. This mess has got to be straightened out.' But I still had no idea how my campaign against Mary's attitude would fare.

"Barbara's school came up again. Mary was no match for the two of us . . . and in September Barbara went to public school.

"She liked it very much. The school was six blocks away, outside of our restricted neighborhood, and the pupils were a 'mixed lot,' as Mary had said.

"Presently Barbara began to tell us about a little girl in her class whose name was Angela Pogachnik. Barbara liked her a lot. She was blonde and had curls like Barbara's. One day they exchanged hair ribbons and thereby became special friends. Mary disapproved of the friendship, but didn't quite know what to do about it.

"Then Barbara started talking about Angela's grandfather, whom Angela loved a lot and whose name was not Pogachnik like Angela's but A-n-t-o-n O-g-r-i-z-e-k—because he was Angela's mother's father and Angela's mother's name before she married Mr. Pogachnik had been O-g-r-i-z-e-k.

"Mr. Anton Ogrizek was a frail old man, but a spell of Indian summer lured him out every day and he waited to walk home from school with Angela. He was, Barbara said, a very funny little old man. He was all bent and gray, and he walked very slowly with a stick, and he loved Angela as much as she loved him, and he laughed a lot, and he had only a few teeth in front of his mouth, and his hands were very big because he had worked hard all his life, and they shook because he was old, and he hardly spoke any English because he was a foreigner from a country called Slovenia. But he understood English and he was wonderful and a lot of fun. 'His back is round, not straight like yours, Daddy, and his skin is like a piece of paper that you squashed in your hand—he is so old. On the way home Angela takes hold of his hand and the hand shakes, but she likes it very much, and she loves him. . . .' There was no end to Barbara's account of the old man.

"Then one evening Barbara interrupted herself and turned to Mary: 'Gee, Mummy, why haven't you got a father like Mr. O-g-r-i-z-e-k, so I'd have a grandfather, so he could meet me after school, so Mrs. Cranston wouldn't have to call for me?'

"Mary looked at me and turned pale. I stared at her. Then she said with an effort, 'I am sorry, darling; my father died long ago—before you were born.'

" 'But, Barbara,' I said, 'you *have* a grandfather because I have a father.'

" 'He didn't die?' asked Barbara quickly.

" 'No. He's still alive,' I said and noticed that Mary was breathless and rigid.

" 'Gee, Daddy, why didn't you tell me! Where is he?'

"I looked at Mary as if to say: here it comes! She was sitting upright, waiting to hear what I would say and afraid of the worst. I knew the crisis was in sight—and perhaps

easy victory. Mary looked as though she would break at
the slightest touch.

" 'Where is he?' demanded Barbara. Her persevering
streak was going strong.

" 'Why, he is in Pennsylvania,' I said, '—in a little town
called Dexter.'

" 'Gee, why didn't you ever tell me?'

"I looked at Mary again and finally replied, 'I didn't
think you'd care.'

" 'Gee—!' said Barbara, bewildered. 'Of course I care.
Just wait till I tell Angela that I have a grandfather too.'
She did a little dance before me and shrieked with delight.
'What is he like, Daddy?'

" 'Oh,' I said, 'he is a funny-looking old man, maybe a
little like your Mr. O-g-r-i-z-e-k.'

" 'Goody-goody!' shrieked Barbara.

"Then I cut loose and, pulling Barbara onto my lap, I
told her about her grandfather. I told her about the little
house he lived alone in, and about the way he cooked his
own meals and mended his own clothes. At the moment
it didn't matter to me that Mary looked as though she were
about to faint.

" 'But why doesn't he live with us?' asked Barbara.

" 'Oh, I don't know,' I stalled. 'He wouldn't like it in
Cleveland.'

" 'Why not?'

" 'He likes it in Dexter because he's lived there a long
time. He is funny that way.'

"Barbara pondered this, then asked, 'How old is he?'

" 'Sixty-two or -three.'

" 'Only sixty-three!' said Barbara. Her grandfather's
youth was a blow. 'Angela's grandfather is seventy-seven.
How much more is that than sixty-three?' I told her to
get a pencil and figure it out; she was not very good at
arithmetic. When she got 14 and my assurance that it was
correct, she said, 'Oh gee!' But in a minute she got over

her disappointment and asked, 'What is my grandfather's name?'

" 'Nick,' I said: 'N-i-c-k.'

" 'N-i-c-k—Nick—Grandfather Nick,' experimented Barbara. 'That's pretty nice. Nick Nichols—his other name is Nichols, isn't it? Like ours?'

"Here I winced a little. 'No,' I said.

" 'But why not? What *is* his name?'

" 'Well,' I said, 'he has a very funny name because he is a foreigner too, like your friend Angela's grandfather.'

" 'Gee, why didn't you tell me! Wait till I tell Angela! What's his name, Daddy? *What's* his name? Tell me quick! I think you're mean. Isn't he, Mummy?' Barbara scarcely glanced at Mary. In her excitement she did not see that her mother sat like a statue, pale and silent. 'What's his name?' demanded Barbara again.

"I laughed and said, 'His name is Sobuchanowsky—Nick Sobuchanowsky.'

" 'Sobuch— How do you *spell* it, Daddy? Write it down for me. Quick. Here: print it—please.'

"I began to print and Barbara called out the letters. Then she said, 'Gee! That's *terrific*! Sobu—Sobuch—Sobuchanowsky! This is much better than O-g-r-i-z-e-k or P-o-g-a-c-h-n-i-k. Wait till I tell Angela. But, Daddy— *Why* is my grandfather's name So-bu-cha-now-sky? Yours is Nichols. Shouldn't they be the same?'

"I said, 'Mine used to be Sobuchanowsky too when I was a boy. Then I changed it to Nichols.'

" 'Why?'

" 'Oh, Sobuchanowsky was too long. People had a hard time with it. Even you have trouble.'

" 'I haven't either,' said Barbara. 'I'll practice saying it and I'll say it as easily as you do. I'll spell it too without looking at the paper. I think it's a shame you changed it.'

" 'Why?' I said.

" 'It just is,' said Barbara.

" 'I think Nichols is a fine name. Anybody can say it or spell it. Don't you like it, Barbara?'

" 'It's all right,' said Barbara. 'But S-o-b-u-c-h-a-n-o-w-s-k-y is wonderful. Sobuchanowsky—see how I can say it? Nick Sobuchanowsky—Barbara Sobuchanowsky! If you hadn't changed your name, Daddy,' she reproached me, 'I'd be Barbara Sobuchanowsky, wouldn't I? Wouldn't I, Mummy? And you'd be Mrs. Sobuchanowsky, the way Angela's mother is Mrs. Pogachnik—wouldn't you, Mummy?'

" 'Yes, darling,' said Mary. Her voice was barely audible.

" 'Sobuchanowsky is *much* better than Pogachnik or Ogrizek,' Barbara continued.

" 'But Barbara,' I said, 'didn't you ever notice my middle initial?'

" '*S.!*' shrieked Barbara. 'It stands for Sobuchanowsky!'

"I nodded while she danced in the middle of the room. Then she said, 'You are John *Sobuchanowsky* Nichols. So if I want to I can be Barbara *Sobuchanowsky* Nichols, can't I?' She looked at Mary, then at me. Then, as there was no objection, she announced: 'That's my name now! Barbara Sobuchanowsky Nichols!'

"I saw Barbara to bed that night. Mary sat on in the living-room. Barbara was too excited to notice how strange she looked. She had even forgotten to kiss her mother good night, perhaps for the first time. I was her hero, for I had supplied her with a grandfather.

"When I returned to the living-room, Mary was still sitting there. She glared at me in a white rage. All of a sudden she got up and rushed into our bedroom. I followed. She looked as though she wanted to throw something at me. Her lips trembled; she trembled all over. Then she said, 'You smug, selfish, weak—!' Her anger choked her; she couldn't go on.

"I seized her arms. She raged speechlessly, trying to get

loose, but I held her. I had to; it was now or never. I said,
'I *have* been weak, Mary—a fool—but so have you—we've
both been fools.' I shook her with all my strength. 'You
started this. I shouldn't have let you, but I did. It's my
fault. And I've *got* to break this whatever-it-is between us.'

"She stood rigid. I shook her again. Her head swung
back, then forward, and she went limp. She slumped on
the bed and broke into tears.

"I hadn't seen her cry since the night I proposed. Something in me spilled over and recaptured my early feeling
for her. She cried like a child ——

"Then we talked. It was simple, easy. It was the first
time we had ever really talked. The taboo was gone, and
all at once all the things between us fell away.

" 'I've been such a fool! Such a fool!' said Mary a dozen
times if she said it once.

"I said I had been worse.

"She said I should have kicked her or something when
she first laid down the 'torn out of the book' arrangement.

"We told each other about all the things we had never
spoken of—about our childhood, our parents, our 'foreign'
names.

"Mary tried to explain, but she had suppressed her early
experiences so thoroughly she had difficulty recalling details. 'Our farm was in Saginaw County where there were
a lot of German farms,' she told me. 'My father was fairly
well-to-do. When the war began some of the Germans were
in favor of the Kaiser, some did not care one way or another, and some were loyal to the United States. My father
was. He was a citizen. . . . Then, in the fall of 1917, our
farm was set on fire. I was only eleven but I remember it
burning. It was in the evening. Father couldn't even get
all the cattle out of the barn. A horse burned, too. I remember the smell. . . . Mother was terribly frightened.
She thought 'they' might kill us. We were 'Huns'—someone

yelled that word from a car that went by a stone's-throw from the blazing house. No one helped us fight the fire. The other German farmers were afraid. So everything just burned down. Father's face and hands were badly burned. He barely saved a colt. His hair was burned away from one side of his head and he looked terrible. For a while there was an awful look in his eyes. Mother was afraid he would go crazy. He laughed as though he were mad when he discovered that the Liberty Bonds he had bought a while before were burned along with his citizenship certificate and some money which he had kept in a tin box. Then he got hold of himself and told us we were leaving. He owned an old Ford, and Mother and he put in it what was left. He sold the colt and a few cattle; the rest he gave away. He did not sell the land, he just left it . . . and we went to Detroit. There we switched from Schwabenland to Land. Mother had never been well; now Father had to put her in a hospital, and she died. . . . I think I had already begun to get rather strange. I crawled into myself and looked out at the world—and cringed. During the war everybody was terribly patriotic and I was scared someone would find out I was a 'Hun.' Of course I wasn't a 'Hun'! I had been born in Michigan. I was an American; of course I was. Father was a citizen even if his papers had been destroyed; and he looked all right, except for the scars on his face and the lack of hair over his right ear. But I hated him. He was German. He was my father. I was all confused. Once or twice I had the horrible idea of reporting him as a German, because people where we lived didn't know he was one. He said he was a Hollander—before coming to America he had sailed on Dutch ships and he spoke a little Dutch. . . . It was humiliating to be supported by him. Yet I liked him too; he was a fine man. He never suspected what was going on inside me and was always good to me. He had a sense of duty and was a hard worker. In Detroit he bought a little cigar-candy-and-newspaper stand, which he kept open from seven in the morning till ten at night. He ran it till he dropped dead of heart failure. . . . I was eighteen then. The money he left me was all in cash in a steel box in his trunk. He had finally sold the farm in Saginaw County. Now I sold his business. I grieved for him, but I was glad to be free at last to be an American. I would make something of myself. I burned everything I found in the box except the money. There was a wedding picture of my father and mother which had somehow survived the fire. I burned it. I wanted to go on from *here*; everything that was past was done for. I was determined to be effective, independent, self-sufficient. The whole thing grew into a complex. . . . When I got the job with Mr. Sumner, it was all the more important that no one should find out I was German. Mr. Sumner is very American. He was an Army officer during the war. He belongs to the Legion. He thinks foreigners are all right in a factory, but he won't have them in his office ——'

"We talked most of the night.

"Pulling down the wall between Mary and me, however, did not terminate our difficulty all at once. Far from it. During the next week Mary relapsed more frequently than I. The firm grip of the old attitude on her whole personality was not easy to break. She was miserable, at times to the point of physical pain. The abrupt and radical change sapped her strength, and she stayed in bed as much as she could. She had fits of weeping. She told me it was often all she could do to keep from breaking down away from home.

"But we had savored the deep pleasure of sincerity. The throwbacks grew less and less frequent. As it affected us three our predicament was resolved; but how about the world immediately around us? Were we going to tell our friends? How? Whom, to begin with? Suddenly we realized

we had no intimate friends . . . and we decided to let developments take their course. This applied to our jobs too.

"I said nothing to Mary but it occurred to me she had
probably needed the activity of her position with Mr.
Sumner to keep busy—to keep going with the 'torn out of
the book' scheme. She would have that problem no longer.
Perhaps she would like to quit her job, especially since
we did not exactly need her salary.

"Barbara was no problem. She was young enough to
slide naturally into our new relationship.

"But Mary worried and fretted about my father. She was
afraid it would be extremely awkward to meet him after
they had been in-laws for over eight years. She clung to
the hope that it might be neither necessary nor desirable.
After all, he was a pretty strange old man. He might not
like her, or she might not like him. But she was conscience-stricken and ashamed of herself.

"We had for some time all but ceased going out and
we did not miss our old crowd. It was clear now that our
social life had been largely a matter of jitters. Neither Mary
nor I cared any longer what any of our friends would think
when they learned we were really 'foreigners.' The postman amused us. One evening we thought of addressing an
envelope to 'Mr. Vassiliy Boulubanoff' in care of us, but
we didn't; it seemed a little silly.

"The day after Barbara heard she had a grandfather
she told the big news to Angela Pogachnik, who was properly impressed. She informed her grandfather, Mr. Ogrizek,
that her friend Barbara Nichols also had a grandfather,
who was even more foreign than he was because his name
was so foreign very few people could pronounce it and
Barbara's father had had to change it to Nichols.

"Barbara told her teacher too and asked her to please
amplify her name to Barbara Sobuchanowsky Nichols in
the school records because she had a grandfather in Penn-

sylvania whose name was Sobuchanowsky and her father's middle initial was 'S.' which stood for 'Sobuchanowsky' and it was her name now.

"A week or so later one of the teachers in my school suddenly hailed me with, 'Hi there, Sobucha—ha-cha—chanowsky!' He was a sort of friend of mine, and was obviously amused. He said there was a good deal of gossip about it in school.

" 'What kind of gossip?' I asked.

" 'Don't let it worry you,' he said. 'I know for a fact that Black's'—the vice-principal's—'name used to be Schwartzengrobber or something like that. Personally, I don't care what anybody's name is or was.'

"But a few of the teachers did care. One or two were our former friends, whose manner now changed considerably. And there was Miss Chickering, an elderly woman, always very aggressive and 'patriotic' in and out of faculty meetings. She was the leader of a kind of clique which had all sorts of things mixed in its cause but which did not include the principal, though he was close to it.

"One day the principal stopped me and asked what was all this about my name being Sobuchanowsky. I didn't like the way he smiled. I explained briefly. And that was all for a while.

"Then I discovered the pupils knew about my name. This was annoying. I couldn't quite define it, but there was a difference in the atmosphere—although I probably imagined some of it. But I mentioned it to Mary. She was upset. I thought I would just put up with it. It was bound to ease off.

"But I was increasingly self-conscious in classrooms. The textbooks we used barely mentioned the New Immigration; America was the result purely of the early settlers. I read a couple of books on immigration, also an essay in a book called *New Viewpoints in American History* by Professor Arthur M. Schlesinger of Harvard.

"My idea about what I'd do was not yet formed, but at a faculty meeting early in November I suddenly spoke up. The point I made was that 'our forefathers,' so stressed in the books we used, were not really the forefathers of a lot of the students. Nor my own, for that matter. 'In a way,' I said, 'we of the newer stocks are pretty much left out when it comes to recounting the stream of history in this country.'

" 'Well, why don't you come in?' retorted the militant head of the clique I mentioned. She glared at me. 'The water is fine.'

"Another teacher, one of the newest in school, spoke up agreeing with me.

"I felt wonderful. I think 'clean' is the word. Now I was not hiding anything any more. I summarized the Schlesinger essay—to the effect that 'foreigners' had taken a considerable part in the creation and development of the United States.

"Miss Chickering made a ten- or fifteen-minute speech so 'flag-waving,' so emotionally confused, that I can't tell you what it meant except that she didn't care what Professor What's-his-name said even if he was from Harvard. America had let the foreigners in and now they could just become Americans or go back where they came from.

"She certainly had some of the teachers with her.

"The principal coldly asked me if there was anything else I wished to say.

"I said no, except that I hoped anyone interested would read the Schlesinger essay.

"As I left the school building that afternoon two more teachers came up to say that I was right. I felt very good in my head and chest, but suddenly very insecure under my feet. It was actually a physical sensation. I wasn't afraid I would be fired. But I suspected that hereafter my job might not be any too pleasant. I am not a fighter. Nor a leader. I never have been. It is hard for me to admit this, but it's the truth. I realized that it was almost unnatural for me to speak out at the meeting. I knew I could not follow it up with anything effective. Besides, who was I? Just a teacher ——

"The next day I wrote to Clark on an impulse asking if he knew of any jobs out West, and if so, how to go about getting one.

"He replied he didn't know of anything offhand, but something might turn up, and he would let me know. He said he was planning to come East at Christmas, and would stop off in Cleveland to see me.

BARBARA AND HER GRANDFATHER
SOBUCHANOWSKY

"Barbara practiced writing and saying her new name. Once in a while she asked when she would see her Grandfather Sobuchanowsky. Why didn't he come to see us?

" 'As I told you,' I said, 'he never goes anywhere. He is a funny old man, you know. Also,' I added, 'he has a job.'

"This was another disappointment to Barbara. She did not say anything for a minute but she evidently thought grandfathers ought not to work; if they did there was something wrong. Then she remembered that her grandfather was only sixty-three to Mr. Ogrizek's seventy-seven; but she had already swallowed this unpalatable fact.

"She asked, 'What does he do?'

" 'He works in a mine.'

" 'In a mine!' Barbara exploded with delight. 'Mr. Ogrizek used to be a miner too! Gee, Daddy, why didn't you tell me?'

" 'I didn't know you'd be interested.'

" 'Of course I am interested!'

" 'Well, I am glad you are,' I said, 'but how should I know? Is there anything else you want to know about your grandfather?'

" 'I want to know *everything*,' said Barbara.

" 'Anything special?' I was having a good time. Mary was enjoying it too.

" 'Special?' said Barbara. 'I want to know everything special—and unspecial too.'

"Barbara laughed with us, although she was not sure what about. Then she demanded a visit to Grandfather Sobuchanowsky. Her idea was we should go at once.

" 'Darling,' said Mary, 'how do you know you will like him?'

"To Barbara this was irrelevant. 'Of course I will like him!' she said.

" 'How do you know he will like you?'

" 'Oh, he will like me all right. Grandfather Ogrizek likes Angela. Why shouldn't Grandfather Sobuchanowsky like me? I am a nice girl, ain't I?'

" '*Am I not*, Barbara.'

" 'Am I not?'

" 'Yes,' said Mary, 'but I wouldn't be too sure. I've never seen him either, and I don't know if he will like me or not.'

" 'Of course he will!' said Barbara.

"Mary and I decided to go to Dexter for Thanksgiving.

"I drove down a day ahead. This was my idea. I wanted to visit Dad alone for the last time; I hardly know why. I found him as usual. He had just got up when I arrived. He was not surprised to see me, although this was the first Thanksgiving I visited him.

"Mary came in her car with Barbara. They brought a turkey and a basketful of things to make a regular Thanksgiving feast—celery, cranberries, nuts, a pumpkin pie and a mince pie too.

"I made Dad lay off a couple of days. At moments before Mary and Barbara came he was beside himself. Then he greeted Mary in his usual matter-of-fact way as though he saw her regularly. She was ill at ease for a while. The old man disturbed her, and the little house was so shabby. But she began to laugh over Barbara.

"Barbara and her grandfather clicked at once. They could not take their eyes off each other. At first he seemed almost afraid to touch her. But he began to look much younger. He bustled about trying to do everything at once. He had to go out on an errand and took Barbara along by the hand. He walked so fast she had to run to keep up with him. They went up the street as though they had been doing it every day for years, he with his long, loose walk, Barbara trotting by his side.

"When they got back Barbara whispered to us: 'He's wonderful, Daddy! Why, Mummy, he's the cutest thing! He's so funny-looking!' That he was so much younger than Mr. Ogrizek and could get around like a monkey began to be an attraction instead of a drawback.

"They had some difficulty in understanding each other's language but they soon got over it. Dad's lack of English was another thing in his favor. On his side he whispered to Mary and me that his granddaughter was 'wunnerfool like sonafhitch.' After the momentary shock Mary almost laughed herself sick. In fact both of us had never laughed so much as on that Thanksgiving Day.

"The visit was a great success. The dinner was a four-way collaboration, but it turned out fine. It was another climax to Dad's triumph: I was an American; I had an American wife and an American child; we ate a real American Thanksgiving dinner.

"When we left, Barbara pulled down Dad's head and kissed him. Tears came into his eyes.

"Barbara raved all the way back to Cleveland.

"We went down again for Christmas and then every six or eight weeks until we went West.

"In school nothing really happened. I had nothing more to say at staff meetings and I was left alone. But I was miserable because I didn't have it in me to force the issue and fight for what I believed. Since I had opened the subject, something was evidently expected of me by the teachers who agreed with me; and I felt all the worse on this account.

"Mary and I discussed the situation. We thought that

maybe my inability to put up a fight came of my summed-up experience as a second-generation American. Mary, not sure anyway whether my idea was worth a fight, thought if I felt unhappy in my position I might resign it. We had some money and were in a position to do a number of things. We might go into business; she had lots of good ideas. I said I liked teaching and told her I had sounded Clark out. Mary liked the idea of going West . . . so I wrote him again, saying I hoped he would be able to give me at least a day in Cleveland.

"He came early in the morning and was with us till late in the evening. He took a great shine to Barbara. When I got him alone I told him my story. It upset him. He said he would never have imagined that a change in name could have such ramifications.

"After Barbara went to bed, we three had a long talk, discussing all the ins and outs of the situation.

"He went on to New York, sent Barbara a present . . . and wired me on New Year's Eve. His train would stop in Cleveland the next morning for twenty-five minutes. Could I meet him at the station? When I saw him he asked me if I had a Ph.D. I said I was working for one at Western Reserve, and he offered me a job at his college. He felt a little to blame for the mess I had got myself into and thought it might be best for Mary and Barbara and me to clear out of Cleveland. One of his men in the History Department had just resigned and he seemed to have no doubt I could fill the vacancy.

"Mary and I decided to accept the offer. We gave up our jobs in Cleveland—with some regret. . . .

"Then we drove West. We have been out here not quite seven months now. I think it was a wise move. College teaching is different, of course, from high-school, but I am getting the hang of it. Next summer I go to Stanford to continue my work for a Ph.D. Bill Clark has been most considerate and helpful; I have no idea how I shall ever repay him. His wife and Mary took to each other too, which makes it very pleasant for us.

"There is one more important item. Dad went with us. That spring the mine company retired with a small pension a lot of its old workers, and Dad was pathetically bereft of occupation. He worried about the water in the mine and hung around the shaft till he became a standing joke.

"We worried about him a good deal.

"Then Barbara settled his future. We discovered she had assumed right along we would take him with us. Mary and I looked at each other and laughed, realizing that Dad was practically West if he wanted to go.

"We offered a few feeble objections. I wondered what he would do in a little college town. Mary worried about where he would live—with us? But Barbara insisted. And there was no real reason against it. So he came too.

"The week before we started I wrote Mike about all this and said I wanted to stop in Pittsburgh with Dad to say good-by to him. I told him when we would be there. But we couldn't find him. He was not at his hotel or his office, and he had left no word. Did he deliberately evade us? I think so. Perhaps he has finally cut loose from us all. I have written him from here; no answer.

"We took two weeks to drive across two-thirds of the continent. I am tempted to tell you a little about the trip —of Dad's matter-of-fact acceptance of Cleveland, Chicago, St. Louis, and the plains and mountains; and of Barbara's delight with the country—but I needn't. We all enjoyed it, although now and then Dad irritated Mary and me. Or perhaps I should say that we were irritated with ourselves over him. He *is* funny-looking. Certainly traveling with us he was a bit of an incongruity; and people looked from him to the rest of us, wondering. We were annoyed at him, at them, and at ourselves. But Barbara's complete acceptance of him helped us over this too.

"We swung around through Southern California so we could see Annie. I had written her from Cleveland, then again from Phoenix, and she knew beforehand when we would arrive. Her husband was not at home.

"Annie was 'nice' to us—in quotation marks. I couldn't make her out. She was nervous. With all the sun in California there was an unhealthy pallor on her face, which seemed flat even when she smiled. Her two oldest children were not home either. She didn't explain their absence. . . . I wondered about her as I looked at her. She had been such a fine, real person as a girl back in Dexter. Now here she was a 'lady' in a big expensive house. I thought she must still be fine; one doesn't just cease to be what one was. But she was not herself. She was uneasy. She must be terribly confused. Was it all her ambitious husband's fault?

"They have a conventional, showy place in Glendale, with palms and lemon-trees in front, and a general appearance of success. Possibly she and Gates are thoroughly happy with each other and she can therefore cut away the past more successfully than we could. Perhaps she is involved in a situation essentially like our old 'torn out of the book' scheme. Maybe we gave her the idea. I don't know, I don't know. Every once in a while I caught her staring at Dad or Mary or Barbara or me. There were sudden silences, then rapid chatter on her part.

"Dad took it all in his stride. He had nothing to say. He grinned a little and sat quietly. It occurred to me that inside him he had more dignity than all of us put together —except Barbara.

"Annie was 'nice' to Dad, but I had a distinct feeling that

she was afraid some of her friends might drop in while we were there. I am sure she was relieved when we left ——

"A word about Joe.

"I am within reach of Tacoma now but I haven't the faintest idea if he is still there, or how to get hold of him. He worries me. I thought he might be working in the big airplane factory there or have something to do with the union. I wrote to both the company and the union. The company replied nobody by the name of Sobuchanowsky worked for them, but there has been no reply from the union. Of course Joe might have drifted up to Seattle or down to San Francisco or Los Angeles—or anywhere. . . .

"It amuses me to remember that we worried about what Dad would do with himself here. I think we were afraid he would be on our hands. But as it turns out, no matter how one looks at him, he doesn't bother anyone; he is not in anybody's way.

"One day shortly after we got here he came upon a great pile of coal beside the heating plant in back of the college. It interested him. He hung around; asked a question or two, I suppose; met the plant superintendent who just then needed someone to keep the furnace going and who took him on. All that Dad needed were a few pointers.

"He lives in the plant. He batches. He still isn't a citizen; he had to register as an alien . . . and on that occasion Bill Clark, who thinks the world of him, made a speech about him in Assembly. Clark explained why some foreigners who have been here a long time never have taken out citizenship papers—because they are simple, timid people, unable to learn sufficient English, or afraid of contact with officialdom, or perhaps incapable of realizing the importance of citizenship, but nonetheless effective as human beings.

"Barbara is Dad's special favorite. He would die as he

now lives for her. He says he will live forever; Barbara keeps him 'yoonk.' He gives her presents. He has started a savings account for her. He wants her to be 'reech.' He has fixed his routine in the heating plant so he can see her home from school.

"My change of name is all right so far as Dad is concerned: I am an American. He listened with interest, then nodded, when I told him I took 'Nichols' because his first name was Nikolai. But he is also delighted that his granddaughter is Barbara Sobuchanowsky Nichols.

"Once a week Dad stays for supper. His manners have greatly improved, thanks to Mary who has taken a lot of trouble with him—not so much to 'reform' them as to keep Barbara's acceptable, for in her admiration she imitates him too much. With all possible tact, Mary explained the problem. He thought it over, understood, and submitted to correction. But he still looks 'funny,' and frankly I am still a little self-conscious about him. People know he is my father, and I am glad there is no secret about it, but I prefer not to be seen with him on the campus or in town. He is so proud over my being a teacher in a 'kulich' that I am afraid his pride attracts too much attention. I am his triumph, the crown of his success as an immigrant. And I, alas! am anything but satisfied with myself—not only as a teacher but as his son. My Cleveland attitude still hangs on, and I am as ashamed of it as I can be, but I can't seem to get rid of it entirely—though I hope that gradually it will leave me. This is true also of Mary, although she genuinely likes Dad. We are glad he is here, glad for his sake and for Barbara's—and, let me add, for the good of my soul.

"So the ending of the story is not completely happy. It is happy for the first and third generations. Dad is all right, all set; for Barbara at eight, the prospects of life are the best. For us of the second generation things are still un-clear. Mary and I are only just beginning to inch into daylight ——

John S. Nichols."

THE END

Appendix: Miscellanea on Names

EDITORIALS: 1942

A number of editorials dealing with names appeared in different newspapers while I was preparing this book. The following three suggest what editorial writers can do in respect to "foreign" names.

From the Boston Globe, *May 6, 1942:*

TALE OF NAMES

The list of 126 New England Navy men who during the first four months of the war have given their lives for their country tells a tale of its own. It is not only that some unknown soldier has sacrificed his life for his nation, his ideals, his faith. Most of them are "unknown" soldiers, though there are their families, their friends, who know their names. The great masses of the people have never heard of them, yet the whole nation salutes those gallant officers and men.

Perhaps an even more inspiring thing about this list are 126 names of Americans, English, Scotch, Irish, French, Polish, Czech, Greek, Lithuanian, many an Italian and one German name. They came from different stock, from different countries. They had different backgrounds, different cultures. They may even have lived as they or their parents used to live, "over there." But they all died as Americans, defending one nation, indivisible, with liberty and justice for all.

Nazi Germany has created a slogan: "One nation, one Reich, one leader." What that meant was a pledge, excluding all other peoples. This nation has practiced a pledge including and embracing all peoples willing to be one in liberty and justice. The 126 New Englanders have confirmed it with their lives. That is the tale of their names.

From the New York Herald Tribune, *May 6, 1942:*

THE CHINESE NAME PUZZLE

In a recent news dispatch from Washington reference was made to Dr. Hu Shih, the Chinese Ambassador to this country. Farther along in the report, when he came up for mention again, he was called Dr. Shih. This happens to be wrong, for this amiable and scholarly diplomat's family name is Hu, and Shih is what we should call his given name. No one could be certain of this, however, until he had been told that it was so; for, while the family name always comes first in China and the given names follow it, many English-speaking Chinese turn their names end for end when dealing with Occidentals, as the Japanese now almost invariably do. Therefore, when each name is a single syllable, as in Dr. Hu's case, there is simply no telling which is the surname.

The commonest practice in China is to have a one-syllable surname and a two-syllable hyphenated given name. Whether a Chinese elects to call himself Wang Ta-tao or Ta-tao Wang, it is fairly safe to assume that his family name is Wang. If he signs himself Wang Ta Tao, however, there is no telling what name he was born with, because both Wang and Tao are possible surnames. Furthermore, there are a limited number of double-barreled surnames in China. They are not very common, however, so that if a gentleman handed you his card with Ssu-ma Lin on it and you called him Mr. Lin, instead of Mr. Ssu-ma as a Chinese would, he would readily forgive you.

There is no space here for a dissertation on the pronunciation of Chinese names, but that is a serious problem to Chinese students in this country, and to solve it they sometimes give themselves names which are meaningless to their fellow countrymen. Suppose a young man from Peiping arrives here with a name like Hsieh Ts'un-jao, as it would be rendered according to the standard Wade system of romanization. None of those three syllables is pronounceable by the untutored American tongue. They are conventionalized spellings of sounds that cannot be represented by our letters as we pronounce them. The unfortunate Mr. Hsieh finds himself virtually nameless until he discovers that his family name sounds something like Shay to his American friends and that this is a family name. He happily becomes Mr. Shay. Still nothing much can be done about Ts'un-jao. But he happens to have a "hao," or label, by which he is intimately known to his Chinese friends. This is Fei-lan. It suggests Frank, and behold he is Frank T. J. Shay, under which masquerade his own mother certainly would not know him, but to which sad travesty upon a noble name his university will probably append M.A. or Ph.D. in due course.

From the Los Angeles Daily News, *March 4, 1942:*

O'SHEA, PROCHASKA, KAZ & CO.

That is the name of an American firm that until recently was doing business in the islands of Wake and Guam. A colorful and picturesque combination. O'Shea, Prochaska and Kaz!

The company is out of commission for the time being, while the Japs extend their thrust southward throughout the Pacific, overcoming resistance by force of overwhelming numbers. But you'll hear these names, or names very much like them before long, for there are thousands of O'Sheas, Prochaskas and Kaz's all over the United States.

O'Shea, Prochaska and Kaz are three names selected at random from the list of gallant soldiers taken prisoner by the cohorts of the Son of Heaven. Somehow the trio suggest a Notre Dame backfield of "Fighting Irish." Or, they might be members of a prosperous law firm.

But to us the important thing they suggest is America. These men are symbols of the land they are defending with their blood because it is a country where it makes no difference whether a man's name be Kaz or Cohen or Montmorency Caswell Blythe-Whittington as far as the essentials are concerned.

O'Shea, Prochaska and Kaz are not Mayflower names, but they speak of many ships from every realm under the sun. These boys' grandfathers and grandmothers pinched and saved their pennies looking ahead to the golden day when they might embark in a crowded steerage and sail to the land of promise.

Here in America their forefathers found what they had dreamed about in a narrow, prejudiced Europe—freedom that exceeded even their deepest longings. So sweet was their escape from repression and tyranny that they were willing to fight to defend for their children the new liberty, and in turn their children are ready to resist with their lives the dangers that now menace America.

The roster of prisoners taken at Wake and Guam speaks more eloquently than a congressman's labored words of what the Star Spangled Banner really means. In our far Pacific outposts Diederich fought beside Terfansky and Zarlonga and Bendenski and Zivko. Japan's Son of Heaven and Germany's Son of Hell look just alike to men such as these.

O'Shea, Prochaska and Kaz carry no banner of racial superiority and hatred. They are the children of freedom fighting for themselves and for the free generations that will be born long after the names of Hitler and Hirohito have reverted to the dust.

TWO ARTICLES

In magazine files I have come upon two articles which seem to me worth reading in connection with this book.
The first is from The Independent, *January 25, 1906*:

WHAT IS YOUR NAME?

By LAURA ALTON PAYNE

Statistician for the Kansas State Superintendent of Public Instruction

Have you ever thought of the meaning of your name? Do you know its origin—Celtic, Teutonic, Latin?

Some names speak for themselves as to origin and meaning, some are merely non-suggestive, while others are wholly misleading. A cursory glance at any list of English surnames is sufficient proof of this. Considering the surprising changes that many names have undergone, the almost universal lack of knowledge concerning their origin is not to be wondered at. What is there in "Peter Snooks" to suggest to the uninitiated that originally it was "Peter at the Seven Oaks"? Though "Thomas Whitehorse" suggests the American Indian custom in names, originally it was "Thomas at the White Horse," or "Thomas at the sign of the White Horse" (a tavern). This was the source of many of the "animal" surnames. In mediaeval times our genial Bill Nye would have been "Bill atten eye"— i.e., "at the island." Niles, Nash, and Noakes had similar origin. How can Sucksmith, Shuxsmith, and Sixsmith be expected to know that a remote ancestor of theirs made sickles, hence was called Skelysmith? Sidney is a corruption of St. Denys, Sinclair of St. Clair, Seymour of St. Maure, Janeway of Genoa, Curtis of "courteous," Armitage of "hermitage," Spark of Sparrowhawk, Turkle of Thorskettle (the sacrificial kettle of the gods also gave rise to the name Cattle), and

Bunyan of Bonjohn—John Bunyan meaning "John Good John." Emerson and America had the same origin—Almeric, an old Norman name, Amerigo being the Italianized form.

Names, like things, are not always what they seem. Beers and Berry are not "beers" and "berry," but a corruption of "borough," often written "bury" and "bery." Badman was not originally "bad," but the opposite, "bead" or "bedeman," he who counted his beads, or rosary, as he professionally invoked heaven in behalf of his patrons. Death and Graves are not so sepulchral as they sound; the former is a corruption of the old Flemish name D'Eath. The latter has the same origin as the word "engrave"—"to carve"—originally applied to a clearing in the forest. Grove now means just the opposite. Chapman was "chepeman," or market man. Waters and Agate are not of "mineral" origin; Waters is a contraction of Walters, and Agate of "atte-gate." Nor is Lambkin of "animal" origin; it does not mean "little lamb," but "little Lambert," from St. Lambert. The original Tallboys was not a giant in his youth; his name is a double place-name, from "tailles" (underwood) and "bois" (wood). "Boys" and Boyce are other forms of "bois." Gotobed was not a sleepy-head; his descendants allowed his fine old Teutonic name, Godbert or Godeberd, to become corrupted. Quarterman does not signify a weakling, but *quatre-main*, "four-handed"; and Potiphar, instead of Bible origin, is a corruption of Pedifer—"iron-footed."

Some fine-sounding names were of very humble origin. The original Calvert (family name of the famous Lords Baltimore, of Maryland) herded calves, hence "calve-herd." Campbell signifies "crooked-mouth" and Cameron "crooked-nose," just as the river Cam was so named because of its winding course. Labouchere is French for "the butcher." Its equivalent, Carnifex, is known in England, Metzger in German, while plain Butcher prevails in America. Durward was "door-ward" and Stewart was "stew-ward." "Stew-ward" was originally "sty-ward"—"sty" signifying "stall" for horses, cows, etc. Stanley was "stone-lea"; Gladstone, "glede-stone"—"crag of the kites, or gledes"; Stoddard, "stot-herd" (stot, A. S. for bullock); and some of our Goddards were "goat-herds." Oliphant is merely a euphonized "elephant."

In the beginning a single personal name sufficed. For awhile no two persons bore the same name, but as a stock of names accumulated repetitions became common, and as the population of the world increased distinctive names became necessary; hence we read of John the Baptist and John the Disciple, Darius Hystaspis and Alexander the Great, Joshua, son of Nun, and Simon Barjonas—"Simon, son of Jonas." As time passed, distinguishing names, given for various reasons, became common among nearly all, if not all, the nations of the earth, but the Roman cognomen was the nearest approach to our modern surname.

The surname is not necessarily the sire-name, or patronymic, as so many people think, though the two are now generally synonymous in use, particularly in the United States and England. The proper orthography of the word is "surname," not "sirname"—"sur" from *super*, signifying "over," i.e., the "over" or additional name. Nor is the surname always inherited. The law recognizes a man's right to choose his own name, even providing for the change by a legislative act. Or a new name may be inherited with a legacy attachment—a custom that still obtains in Scotland and is not infrequent in the United States.

Surnames were first used in France, becoming general there during the latter part of the tenth or the forepart of the eleventh century. They were used hereditarily to some extent, however, prior to that time. They were introduced into England at the Norman Conquest in the year 1066, but it required two or three centuries to establish the body of our nomenclature on a fixed basis. During that time surnames became general throughout the British Isles except in Wales, in some parts of which they are unknown to this day.

It is difficult to trace a pedigree back further than the thirteenth century, owing to a certain easy custom that sprang into use—that of the sons laying aside the father's name and taking one of their own choice from their residence, occupation, or other reasons, brothers frequently choosing different names. All of this was very confusing, but perhaps not more so than that of the present Scandinavian custom, under which the son of John Peterson may become Eric Johnson, whose son in turn may become Peter Ericson, the latter's son probably returning to the original name—John Peterson.

Surnames are now general in all civilized countries, I believe, except Turkey, in which country it is said that a man has no relatives, since he cannot trace them. In England alone there are from 40,000 to 50,000 existing surnames. In proportion to the population, Scotland has fewer surnames than England. Doubtless this is partly due to the adoption, in some instances, of the clan name by the whole clan. Owing to their crudity, inconvenience, or uncomplimentary origin, many of the early surnames have become obsolete: such as Withoutentown (without the town), Swetinbed, Smartknave, Saucemaker, and Lamentation. Not all such names are obsolete, however. Only recently the writer came across the names Goforth, Goforward, Godbehere, and Wellbeloved. Over 200 names collected by the writer from newspapers, magazines, and catalogs might better have been allowed to fall into "innocuous desuetude," among them the following: Turnipseed, Legliter, Sickendick Dickensheets, Quartermouse, Oldfather, Younghusband, Webfoot, Redhair, Hedgepatch, Tindeer, Stickhorse, Sick, Colic, Meales, Demon. Even the well-known Poindexter loses its dignity in the original Pointdexter.

In most countries it is customary for the wife to take the husband's name, but in some European countries it is not unusual for the husband to append the wife's name, particularly when it is more honorable than his own. Hyphenated names and the wife's retention of her maiden name for a middle name are customs growing in favor in the United States and Great Britain. In Spain the wife retains her own name, and the son may choose the name of either parent, or he may combine the two names. In the former case the son is likely to choose the name that confers the most honor. This custom has obvious merit—obnoxious and dishonored names may be relegated to oblivion, euphonious and honored names perpetuated. When the Spaniard unites his parents' names they are connected by a "y," signifying "and," the father's name being the first and most important, the mother's name being appended chiefly to distinguish father and son, as the terms *senior* and *junior* are unknown in Spain. For instance, the father's name may be Juan Blanco y Alvarez and the son's Juan Blanco y Diaz.

American surnames were determined by the colonization of the country, hence are chiefly of a triple source—English, French, and Spanish, the English consisting of Anglo-Saxon and Norman-French (the former Teutonic and the latter half Teutonic) and Celtic. The purely Teutonic, introduced by the Dutch of New York, has increased greatly by immigration. The great foreign influx is rapidly adding two more important elements—Latin and Slavonic. It is not uncommon for a foreigner with a polysyllabic name to drop part of it upon his arrival here. Occasionally there is a complete change—an "off" or a "ski" becoming by voluntary adoption plain Smith or Jones. As a rule, Scandinavians drop their peculiar custom in names (that of adding "son" to the father's personal name to form the son's surname) along with other old world customs that do not readily naturalize, for, of all foreigners, Scandinavians are the most eager to become Americanized.

Surnames have been drawn from every available source— personal names, location, occupation, deeds of prowess, mental, moral and physical attributes, terms of relationship, the human body, farm and household articles, buildings, foods and drinks, modes of travel, nations and laws, customs and religions, geographical terms, weather and seasons, months and days, measures and values, the joys and ills of life, the animal, mineral and vegetable kingdom, and even from the Kingdom of Heaven. The use of nicknames and compound terms gave an almost inexhaustible source. Even oaths be. came embodied, as in Pardoe, from *par Dieu*. Words were clipped, elided, lengthened, blended and corrupted. Elisions were more common than additions. Augustine became Austin; Cheeseborough, Chesbro; Elias, Ellis; and Taliaferro, Tolliver and probably Dolliver. Dolliver may be a corruption of D'Oliver. Some names have retained their old-style orthography, others have taken the new. Norse words were "Frenchified," French words Anglicized, and British words Latinized. Also, many old Anglo-Saxon and Celtic terms, otherwise obsolete, have been preserved in surnames.

Bardsley, in his *English Surnames*, summarizes the foregoing sources of our English nomenclature under the following head-ings: Baptismal names, patronymics and metronymics, place-names, office and occupation names, and *sobriquets* consisting of nicknames and pet-names. Place-names undoubtedly rank first in number; baptismal names, with their numerous "nicks" and "pets," second; occupation names, third.

Among the Anglo-Saxon names that preceded and survived the Conquest may be mentioned Aldred, from which came our Aldrich; Sigward ("sig," Teutonic for "conquest"), origin of Seward and Sigsby; Swain, or Swan, signifying "strength"; Harding, which has come down to us unchanged; and Here-ward, ancestor to Howard and Harvard. One authority gives Hereward as a corruption of "hayward." But may not its origin be the same as Sigward, since "here" signifies "war"—"heriot," "a tribute for war purposes"?

Names derived from Teutonic mythology were also among the earliest: "god" (good) is found in Goodwin and Godard (one class); Os, in Oswald and Osborne; Thor, in Thustan and Thurlow; Orm (Pagan serpent god), in Orme and Ormsby.

Among the earliest names introduced and confirmed by the Conquest were found Serl, Drew, Bryce, Harvey, Arnold ("ern"—eagle), Albred (now known as Albert and Allbright), Almeric, Ingelram, Ebrardus (Everard), Warim (Guerin, now Warren), Ivo, Hamon (Hammond), and Payn (originally Pagan). After their adoption as surnames the most of these became obsolete as personal names.

Other personal names that lost none of their popularity as such, while giving rise to a long list of surnames were Guy, Ralph (Rawlins and Randle), Charles, Roland, Oliver, Robert, Richard, Roger, Reginald (Reynolds), and Miles, or Milo.

The most popular personal names since the Domesday Book recorded them have been John and William, but their deriva-tives are too numerous to mention here. Roger, Robert, and Richard, took a double nickname in H and D, hence Hodge and Dodge, Hobbs and Dobbs, Hicks and Dicks, with the rougher forms of the last—Higgs and Diggs, and even Hitch, giving rise to Dickens, Hitchcock, and Higginson. Higgin-bottom may mean "Higgin's lowland," but one authority as-cribes it to "itchin," the mountain ash.

Diminutive and other affixes served an important part in the origin of surnames from personal names. The Anglo-Saxon "kin" and "cock" and "ing" are represented in Jenkins, "little John"; Hitchcock, "little Richard," and Browning, "little Brown"; the Norman "ot" and "et," in Eliot, "little Elias," and Emmet, "little Emma" (sometimes "lot" and "let"; Hamlet, "little Hamon"); the French "on" and "en" in Marion and Dickens. Later came "ie" and "ey," as in Ritchie and Willey. The Anglo-Saxon terminal "ish," in Standish, signifies "born of."

Many prefixes were used. The Celtic "Mac" or "M," of the Scotch; "Mc" of the Irish; "Map," "Ap," or "P" of the Welsh, and the Norman "Fitz" (Latin *fils*), signify "son" or "son of," and the Irish "O," "grandson of," McDonald means "son of Donald"; McPherson, "son of the parson." ApRichard, "son of Richard," eventually merged into Pritchard. In some instances, P was corrupted into B—Barry, Bowen. Fitzroy means "son of the king," and Fitz itself is a surname. O'Brian means "grandson of Brian."

There were prefixes to place-names also. The Norman "De" or "Du," the German "Von," and the Dutch "Van," signifying "of" or "from" an estate or place, was used by the nobility, and "at," "atte," or "atten," as in Atwood, Atterbury, or merely the local name, as Wood, by men in humble walks of life. "At" is shortened to "a" in Thomas a Becket—"Thomas at the Brook." The French "La" signifies "the"—Lamont, "the mountain." In Delafield we find "De" and "La" combined. "Saint" is a Norman prefix.

Suffixes are more numerous than prefixes, but, with the exception of "son" and the diminutives, chiefly in place-names. An old couplet says:

> "In *ford*, in *ham*, in *ley*, in *ton*,
> The most of English surnames run."

Other popular terminals are man, field, land, burn, brook, street, and love. The Scandinavians write the terminal "sen" instead of "son," and the Welsh use the genitive—the source of all the seemingly plural names, as Owens, "Owen's son."

Owens, Evans, Johns, Jones, Hanks, Jenks, Johnson and Jansen are the same.

A slight knowledge of old Celtic and Teutonic terms simplifies many names. The Anglo-Saxon "ton" means "town"; Benton signifies "mountain town"; Norton and Sutton, "north town" and "south town." The Danish "by" also means "town"—Kirby (Kirkby), "church town." Coningsby and Kingston are the same. Winthrop (Whinthrop) signifies "furzevillage"; Burham "brook home"; Heathcote, "heath cottage"; Auburn, "old brook"; Beverly, "beaver field"; Berkeley, "birch lea"; Bradford, "broad ford."

Some names apparently plain are misleading, owing to different meanings of a word, not only in different languages, but in the same language. Winchester (Latin *castra*) signifies "camp of victory," but Winslow (Whinslow) means "furze-hill." In some instances "worth" means "value," in others "farmstead" or "dwelling"; Woodworth, "dwelling in the woods"; Kenilworth, "manor on the canal." Kilpatrick means "church of Patrick"; Schuylkill, "hidden creek." The suffix "ing" in Browning means "off-spring," but in Ruddington it means "meadow"—Rud(d)ing-ton, "red-meadow-town."

Many of these surnames are centuries old, and are found in the oldest records—Domesday Book and Hundred Rolls. The trade of weaving has been carried on in England since the thirteenth or fourteenth century by a Sussex (South Saxon) family named Webb. But many others are of a more recent date. . . .

Upon gaining their freedom, the surnameless slaves generally adopted their master's names, hence the prevalence of time-honored names among the colored race. The Chinese place the surname first. Prince Li Hung Chang, if plain "Mister," would be "Mr. Li."

As to the pronunciation of a name, a man may spell his name Smith and pronounce it Jones, if he so desires, and none can say him nay.

A fair knowledge of English nomenclature gives a fair knowledge of English history, so closely are the two interwoven; hence, the former being like the latter—voluminous, it is impossible to give in one brief article more than the merest insight into the subject.

From Scribner's, *September, 1908:*

WHAT'S IN A NAME?

For a man of letters a strong name of striking originality is a precious possession; it is a pearl beyond price, the attainment of which is well worth a resolute effort. An author is fortunate if it is given to him by descent and by baptism— John Milton for example, or Francis Parkman, names combining vigor with a certain distinction. He is lucky if he can achieve it by arbitrary suppression of a superfluous given name, as Bret Harte did and Mr. Rudyard Kipling. He is even justified, if he manufactures it for his own need as Josh Billings did and Artemus Ward. And it is difficult to chide the songster of Sierras when he cast away the Cincinnatus H.— whatever the H. may have portended—which had been inflicted on him by his godparents. After all, Joaquin Miller is more like the name of a poet than ever Cincinnatus H. Miller could have been. Even though poets must be born, their names can be made, if the intending poet knows how to go about it and if he has the courage of his convictions.

Lowell did not hesitate to express his belief that Keats was sadly handicapped by his name. "You cannot make a good adjective out of Keats—the more pity," he declared; "and to say a thing is *Keatsy* is to contemn it. Fortune likes fine names," and "Fame loves best such syllables as are sweet and sonorous on the tongue." There is a noble stateliness in *Miltonic,* a restful dignity in *Spenserian,* and a distinguished lordliness about *Tennysonian.* Beside these lofty adjectives, poor *Keatsy* trembles into insignificance. Even *Burnsy* is better than *Keatsy,* pitiable as it is in itself—pitiable and yet harshly sibilant. And what is the adjective that describes the cunning craftsmanship of Alexander Pope. Is it *Popeian?*—a monstrous vocable; or is it *Papal?* Nor is Poe any better off in this respect; the most one can do is to make shift with *Poe-like,* an unsatisfactory subterfuge.

It is in this same essay on his favorite Keats that Lowell suggested that when the fairies came with their gifts to the cradle of the born poet, one of them, wiser than the rest, should "choose a name for him from which well-sounding derivatives can be made, and best of all, with a termination in *on*." But even a termination in *o* will serve on occasion, and *Platonic* is as elevated a title as *Napoleonic*. It is in another essay of his, on another of his favorites, Walton, that Lowell recurs to this thought and asks "how should Brown or Smith or any other dingy monosyllable of Saxon indistinction compete for conjuration with Pelopidas or Timoleon? Even within living memory Napoleon had a prodigious purchase in his name alone, and prettily confirmed the theory of Mr. Shandy." Indeed, Napoleon is a style and title that swells imperially. Beside it how thin and watered is the name of his pinchbeck nephew, Louis Napoleon. Perhaps it was because they could not deny the loud-sounding majesty of *Napoleon* that the British opponents of the Corsican adventurer, a hundred years ago, insisted on calling him *Buonaparte*.

Besides being sonorous a man of letters, whether a poet or a prose-man, is blest when his name is also aggressively individual, when it belongs to him and indicates him, and him alone, and no one else. Is it mere fanciful association that makes us feel the eternal fitness of the stalwart Mark Twain to the beloved septuagenarian who has made it a household word? Is it merely an *ex post-facto* discovery that Rudyard Kipling is exactly the name that ought to belong to the author of the *Jungle Book*, and that Rider Haggard is exactly the name that ought to belong to the author of *King Solomon's Mines*? For some of us it will be a sad day when the ex-pilot no longer marks twain and when the rudyards cease from Kipling.

It is a misfortune for a man of letters to be born with a dingy Saxon monosyllable for his name, it is a double misfortune if he has to share both of his names with some other seeker after fame. Smiths and Browns there are plenty, and of an inexpugnable indistinction—but Sidney Smith and Sir Thomas Browne managed to snatch victory from prenatal defeat. Even with a dingy monosyllable something may be achieved, from time to time, but what misfortune and disaster follow fast and follow faster a couple of men who have only one name between the two of them! There is a certain American man of letters with leanings toward politics who has the same names, family and Christian both, as a certain British politician with leanings toward literature. Who shall distinguish Dromio of New Hampshire from the Dromio of Birmingham? As the American girl in Paris said after she had matched her own hair with a borrowed braid, *On ne peut pas dire qui est qui.*

THE THIRD OF A SERIES

What's Your Name? is the third of a group of independent books collectively known as The Nation of Nations Series —using a phrase by Walt Whitman: "Here is not a nation, but a teeming nation of nations." The first was *From Many Lands* (1940), the second, *Two-Way Passage* (1941).

In view of certain considerations which have to do with the war and the whole world crisis, I have decided to postpone the publication of *Plymouth Rock and Ellis Island,* which I began to write in the spring of 1941 and then laid aside for *Two-Way Passage.* At the moment I don't know what the fourth book will be. Possibly a sequel to *Two-Way Passage,* sometime in '43.

I continue to welcome reactions to *Two-Way Passage* and shall be grateful for comments on *What's Your Name?*

Louis Adamic,
Milford, New Jersey.

ACKNOWLEDGMENTS

IN THE preparation of *What's Your Name?* I had the aid of a great many people. The names of some of them appear in the text. My deepest thanks to them and others. I owe special gratitude to John A. Rice, Charlotte Morris, Henry Davidson, my assistant Isabel Mangold, and to my wife Stella who have actually worked on the script and/or the proofs.

My thanks, too, to H. L. Mencken for his permission to quote from *The American Language*, to *The New Yorker* for the use of the cartoon on page 129, and to Elias Tobenkin for his piece "Why I Would Not Change My Name."

L. A.